AMERICAN HISTORY IN 90 MINUTES

The Clear, Concise, and Common-Sense Guide to American History

✶ ✶ ✶

©2018 by Anders Odegard. All Rights Reserved.

www.Historyin90.com

CONTENTS

1. Exploration and Settlement 1
2. The Seeds of Revolution 12
3. The American War of Independence 20
4. The Birth of a Nation 30
5. 1800-1860: The Nation Grows..40
6. The Roots of Civil War 56
7. The American Civil War 63
8. 1865-1900 74
9. 1900-1932: Reform, Normalcy, and Depression 84
10. 1933-1945: The Roosevelt Years 94
11. 1946-1980: The Cold War..109
12. 1981-Present: Reagan to Trump 123

Appendix I: The Declaration of Independence..141

Appendix II: The U.S. Constitution 145

EXPLORATION AND SETTLEMENT

It is believed the first inhabitants of the Americas arrived 12,000 to 15,000 years ago by crossing what is now known as the Bering Strait which separates Alaska from Siberia. Over thousands of years the descendants of these early immigrants spread southward and settled in North, Central, and South America. Those settling in North America tended to gather in smaller, scattered communities, while those settling in Central and South America were grouped in more centralized societies such as the Aztec and Mayan civilizations of southern Mexico and the Inca civilization of South America. By 1492 there were millions of these native Americans, most of whom lived in Central and South America.

European Exploration: The first known Europeans to discover the Americas were the Scandinavians. Setting sail from his base in Iceland Scandinavian Leif Eriksson reached the coast of Newfoundland in the early eleventh century A.D. Archeological finds at L'Anse aux Meadows in northern Newfoundland indicate the Scandinavians established a settlement in North America but eventually abandoned it. Scandinavian journeys to North America were limited and by the mid-eleventh century they had ceased entirely.

Christopher Columbus: In the summer of 1492 an Italian sailing on behalf of the Spanish Crown, Christopher Columbus, launched a three-ship expedition into the uncharted waters of the Atlantic Ocean. In one sense the expedition was a failure as Columbus never reached Asia, his desired destination. Yet, in another sense the expedition was a grand success for in October 1492 Columbus landed on an island he called San Salvadore in the present-day Bahamas. Although Columbus was not the first European to set foot on the Americas, his discovery marked the beginning of a steady European presence in the New World.

The Spanish: The Spaniards took the early lead in exploring and conquering the Western Hemisphere. The discovery of gold brought the Spanish conquistadors to the Americas in the early sixteenth century. Conquistadors Hernando Cortes and Francisco Pizarro conquered the Aztec Empire of Mexico and the Inca Empire of Peru. The conquistadors killed and enslaved the natives and returned to Spain with vast quantities of confiscated gold. In the north Spaniard Juan Ponce de Leon became the first known European to explore what is now the continental United States in April 1513. He was followed by Hernando de Soto and Francisco de Coronado, both of whom attempted and failed to find gold and conquer the North American natives. In 1565 Spaniard Pedro Menendez de Avilés founded the first permanent European settlement in North America at St. Augustine, Florida; however, by that time the focus of Spanish exploits was the more profitable Mexico and South America.

The French: The economic success enjoyed by Spain in the early sixteenth century aroused French interest in the Americas. In 1524 Giovanni de Verrazano, an Italian sailing for the French, discovered New York Harbor. In 1534 Frenchman Jacques Cartier discovered the St. Lawrence River in a land he termed "Canada." In 1608, on the banks of the St. Lawrence River, Samuel de Champlain founded Quebec, the first permanent French settlement in the Americas. Quebec gave the French a foothold in Canada and served as a base for a lucrative fur trade with the Indians. Quebec also served as a launch point for subsequent French expeditions into the interior of the continent. In 1673 French explorers Father Jacques Marquette and Louis Joliet discovered the upper Mississippi River. In 1682 explorer Robert de LaSalle journeyed from the upper Mississippi to the Gulf of Mexico and claimed the surrounding territory for France, calling it *Louisiana* in honor of the French Monarch, Louis XIV.

Although the French were avid explorers and made vast territorial claims, their presence in North America was limited by the actual number of Frenchmen inhabiting the continent. The French were interested in America for trading purposes but were not interested in settling in the New World. By the middle of the eighteenth century the French would be far outnumbered by the British in North America. This disparity in numbers would enable Britain to remove forcibly its rival from North America in the mid-eighteenth century.

The Dutch: In 1609 the Dutch East India Company sent explorer Henry Hudson to North America. In September of that year Hudson sailed into New York Harbor and up what is now known as the Hudson River. Dutch traders followed, establishing trading posts on Manhattan and up the Hudson River at Albany. In 1626 Dutch colonist Peter Minuit "purchased" the island of Manhattan from local Indians for goods worth about 60 Dutch guilders, the equivalent of $24. The Dutch settlement on Manhattan became known as New Amsterdam. The Dutch controlled region along the banks of the Hudson River from Manhattan to Albany became known as New Netherland. New Netherland remained under Dutch control until September 1664 when a British naval blockade led by Colonel Richard Nicolls forced Dutch governor Peter Stuyvesant to surrender the colony. Subsequently Nicolls renamed the colony New York in honor of the Duke of York who was sponsoring his expedition. Going forward the official Dutch presence in North America was minimal.

The British: Britain, which would become the dominant power in North America, launched its first exploration of the Americas in 1497. In that year explorer John Cabot sailed down the coast of Newfoundland and claimed the area for Britain. The first substantive British attempt at colonization occurred in 1585 when English gentleman Sir Walter Raleigh sent an expedition to settle on Roanoke Island, just off the North Carolina mainland. The previous year Raleigh had sent an expedition to scout the area and, based on reports from his men, had named the region Virginia in honor of Queen Elizabeth I, the "Virgin Queen." Raleigh's settlers remained on Roanoke for less than a year. When British explorer Sir Francis Drake landed on the island in 1586, the settlers jumped at his offer to return them to Britain. Raleigh sent a second expedition, of whom he hoped were more steadfast settlers, to Roanoke in the summer of 1587. When an expedition arrived on the island in 1590 to resupply these settlers, no trace of the so-called "Lost Colony" was found.

Jamestown: In May 1607 105 colonists founded the first permanent British settlement in the Americas at Jamestown, Virginia. The first few years at Jamestown were extremely difficult. Over half the settlers died the first winter, as they found themselves ill-prepared for the rigors of wilderness survival. Eventually one of the settlers, John Smith, assumed leadership of the community. Smith successfully negotiated aid from the local Indians to help the colonists through the first crucial years. He put the colonists to work, planting corn and building dependable shelter. Smith made the colony somewhat more self-sufficient but still Jamestown remained largely dependent on British supply ships for its survival. The winter of 1609-1610 was particularly brutal. The colony's population, which had grown to 500 that fall, was reduced to just 60 the following spring by starvation and disease. As the colonists were preoccupied with trying to survive day to day, investors in Britain, who were financing the Jamestown expedition, began to grow dismayed by the colony's inability to produce any positive economic return.

Tobacco: The plug might have been pulled on Jamestown had it not been for colonist John Rolfe and tobacco. In 1612 Rolfe harvested the colony's first tobacco crop. Rolfe discovered the Virginia soil and climate to be particularly well suited to the growing of tobacco. Soon the entire colony became engaged in the raising and export of tobacco. Tobacco served to appease the investors in Britain and ensured the continued existence and growth of the Jamestown colony.

The House of Burgesses: In 1619 the Virginia House of Burgesses convened for the first time in Jamestown. Elected by the white males of the colony, members of the House of Burgesses played an active role in assisting the appointed governor of the colony form government policy. The House of Burgesses was the first example of representative government in North America. It provided a model for subsequent North American colonies as they would undergo the task of designing their own governments.

The Pilgrims: In 1620 religious separatists, led by William Bradford and William Brewster, founded a second British colony at Plymouth, Massachusetts. Outcasts in their native Britain, the Pilgrims jumped when given the opportunity to emigrate to Virginia. When their boat, the *Mayflower*, landed quite a bit to the north of Virginia at Plymouth, Massachusetts, the colonists elected to settle there rather than continue their journey. Since these settlers from the *Mayflower* were isolated, they formed their own rudimentary government as outlined in the Mayflower Compact.

The Mayflower Compact gave each of the male colonists a voice in running the new colony.

The Massachusetts Bay Colony: The Plymouth settlers remained in relative isolation for about a decade. Then in 1630 other religious separatists known as Puritans began to migrate to Massachusetts en masse. Under King Charles I, religious tolerance in Britain reached historic lows in the late 1620s and early 1630s. The Puritans found themselves compelled to leave Britain so that they might freely practice their religion. In June 1630, a group of about one thousand Puritans led by John Winthrop landed at Salem, just north of what is now Boston. These Puritans established several settlements in and around the Boston area. Collectively these settlements became known as the Massachusetts Bay Colony. Between 1631 and 1640 the Massachusetts Bay Colony attracted an additional 15,000 to 20,000 immigrants.

The Growth of the British Colonies: The pace of British migration to the colonies quickened in the late seventeenth century. At first the immigrants settled mainly in the Boston area of what became known as New England and the Jamestown area of Virginia, but soon settlements were springing up throughout New England, in the mid-Atlantic states, and in the South. By 1700 about 250,000 colonists lived in what is now the continental United States. These colonists were predominantly of British descent.

Puritanism and the New England Colonies: Puritanism pervaded all aspects of the lives of those who lived in the Massachusetts Bay Colony in the mid-1600s. The Puritan Church ran the government and Puritan ideals for human behavior became civil law. The Puritan leaders, who had come to America to escape religious intolerance in Britain, would not tolerate others in their community who did not share their religious views. Religious dissenters were punished, banished from the colony, and even killed.

Roger Williams: A Salem, Massachusetts clergyman, Roger Williams, openly criticized the Puritan system and the church leaders. Williams preached tolerance for those with alternative religious views and advocated the separation of church and state. The Puritan leaders ordered Williams banished from the Massachusetts Bay Colony in 1635. In 1636 Williams and his followers established a new settlement in Providence, Rhode Island. The Rhode Island colony became a haven for people of all religious views.

The Salem Witch Trials: As the seventeenth century progressed the Puritan Church began losing influence in New England. The expanding trade economy caused New Englanders to begin focusing on economic as well as religious issues. Trade also brought more non-Puritans to New England. Finally the 1692 Salem witch trials, which brought about the executions of 19 people accused of witchcraft, turned public opinion against the harsh, fanatical, and irrational aspects of Puritanism. By the turn of the century Puritanism had lost its grip on New England.

New York: The religious fanaticism which gripped New England in the mid and late seventeenth century stood in contrast to the social liberalism which developed in the Middle Colonies. Under Dutch rule New Netherland and especially New Amsterdam attracted not only settlers of Dutch origin, but Frenchmen, Scots, and Englishmen as well. The Dutch did not attempt to impose a single religion or belief system on the population. When the British overthrew the Dutch in New Netherland in 1664, the Duke of York, who would later become James II, King of England, decided against limiting the social freedoms of the colonists. New Amsterdam, which would grow to become New York City, remained a culturally diverse settlement.

Pennsylvania: The colony of Pennsylvania was born from the vision and efforts of William Penn. The son of a prominent admiral, Penn was reared as a member of England's elite social class. As a student at Oxford College in England, Penn came into contact with and adopted for himself the ways of Quakerism. The Quakers were Christians who spurned the conventions of organized religion. They believed an individual's relationship with God was personal and private. The Quakers also believed in letting others worship and live in the manner they saw fit. In 1681 King Charles II granted the territory which would become known as Pennsylvania to William Penn as payment of a debt owed by the Crown to the Penn family. Immediately Penn went to work recruiting settlers for his new American territory. In the late seventeenth and early eighteenth centuries Pennsylvania grew, attracting Quakers and others from all over Europe. Like Rhode Island, Pennsylvania became a model of democracy and toleration of others.

The Southern Colonies: Widespread growth also swept through the South in the late seventeenth and early eighteenth centuries. Tobacco continued to attract new settlers to Virginia and to the region which became known as North Carolina. Maryland, established in 1632 by Sir George Calvert as a sanctuary for British Catholics, attracted Catholics and Protestants alike with the promise of free land. Founded in 1670 Charleston, South Carolina became the cultural and commercial center of the early South. Finally in 1733 the colony of Georgia was founded. The brainchild of English gentleman James Oglethorpe, the colony of Georgia was designed to give selected residents of Britain's many debtor prisons a chance for a new life in the New World.

The Colonial Economy: The early inhabitants of New England made their livings as farmers. Over time the growing New England population coupled with the limited supply of suitable farmland pushed many New Englanders toward alternative occupations. The distillation of rum became a mainstay industry in New England in the early eighteenth century. Importing molasses from the West Indies, the New Englanders distilled the molasses into rum for export to Britain. Additionally, the bountiful marine life in the North Atlantic off the coast of New England supported a vibrant fishing industry. Other prominent New England industries included lumber production and shipbuilding.

Unlike New England, the Middle Colonies were blessed with an abundance of fertile farmland. Pennsylvania was particularly successful in attracting immigrant farmers and became America's first "breadbasket." Pennsylvania exported its wheat and corn to the West Indies, Britain, and the other colonies. Philadelphia became a bustling port town and Pennsylvania's gateway to the world.

As the seventeenth century turned to the eighteenth century in Virginia and North Carolina, tobacco continued to serve as the region's economic backbone; however, overproduction and resulting low tobacco prices had driven many small farmers out of business in the latter half of the seventeenth century. Replacing the small farms were large tobacco plantations. A typical tobacco plantation was run by a single owner whose family occupied the manor or central house of the plantation. Surrounding the manor were smaller buildings housing the plantation's white workers and black slaves. The plantation system effectively created three distinct economic and social classes in the South: the wealthy educated white owners, the poor landless white foremen and craftsmen, and the black slaves.

The production of rice and indigo made South Carolina one of the richest colonies by the middle of the eighteenth century. Indigo, a plant used in the production of dyes for the textile industry, was introduced into the colony in 1740 and created an instant economic boom. As in Virginia and North Carolina the plantation became the primary vehicle for agricultural production.

Slavery: African slaves were first introduced into the British colonies in 1619 at Jamestown. For most of the seventeenth century African slaves constituted a relatively small portion of the colonial population and were spread evenly throughout the northern as well as the southern colonies. As the plantation system grew to dominate the southern economy during the eighteenth century, demand increased dramatically for slave labor in the South. Additionally, the 1793 invention of the cotton gin greatly increased the importance of cotton production in the South. Unfortunately, a cotton gin alone was not enough to make an early nineteenth century plantation owner wealthy. A large pool of cheap labor was also necessary. The cotton gin ensured that slavery would survive in the South up until the time of the Civil War.

The American Indians: The first British settlers in North America soon realized they were not alone in the New World. Both the settlers in Jamestown, Virginia and the Pilgrims in Plymouth, Massachusetts benefited tremendously from their early contacts with the local natives who became known as American Indians (although Jamestown's Indian relations wavered from friendly to quite antagonistic). The Indians helped the settlers to grow their own food and become familiar with the surrounding landscape. Had it not been for these Indians both colonies would have likely starved and died.

Unfortunately for the Indians the survival of these early colonists encouraged other Europeans to migrate to North America. As the number of these settlers increased, their demand for land also increased. Consequently the Indians, who had occupied these lands for thousands of years, were no longer looked upon as friends but as hindrances to progress. By the mid-seventeenth century the transplanted Europeans were committed to the subjugation and the removal of the American Indian.

The Indians would not go down without a fight. For the next 250 years the North American Indians would adopt both nonviolent and violent means of protecting themselves and their homelands. Nevertheless, in the end the numerical and technological superiority of the European-Americans would prove insurmountable to the American Indian.

THE SEEDS OF REVOLUTION

By the mid-eighteenth century, Britain's economic relationship with its North American colonies was quite substantial. Under terms of the **Navigation Acts**, passed in the latter part of the seventeenth century, Britain enjoyed several advantages in its trade with the colonies. Under the Navigation Acts only British ships were allowed to transport goods imported into and exported out of the colonies. The Navigation Acts stipulated that certain colonial goods, such as indigo and tobacco, be exported only to Britain. Also the colonists were required to purchase certain products only from British manufacturers. This trade relationship was clearly advantageous to Britain. Consequently protecting this relationship from any unforeseen disruption became paramount to Britain's ruling class.

The French and Indian War: As the population of the British colonies along the East Coast increased a growing number of settlers traveled west into the interior of North America to stake their own claims. This migration worried the French who subsequently increased their military presence in the interior of the continent to protect their land claims. This military build-up led to war, the French and Indian War, which pitted the British and the colonists against the French and their Indian allies. From 1754 to 1757 the French and Indian War was waged indecisively. In 1757 William Pitt rose to power in Britain and brought vigor into the British war effort. Pitt appreciated the value of North America to Britain, sparing no expense to drive the French from the continent. By 1760 the British Army and Navy with the help of the colonists had subdued the French military in North America. In the 1763 Treaty of Paris, France renounced its North American territorial claims east of the Mississippi River to Britain. French claims west of the Mississippi went to Britain's ally Spain.

The end of the French and Indian War marked the high point in Britain's relationship with its American colonies. Defeating the French required cooperation between the British and the colonists. The thrill of victory was felt by all. In the early 1760s, colonists were proud to call themselves loyal subjects of King George III, the British Monarch.

Britain's victory in North America did not come without a cost. Burdened with a heavy war debt and the increased costs of running an expanded empire in North America, the British government looked to the colonists to pay a larger portion of the bill.

The Sugar Act: In April 1764 the British Parliament, prompted by Prime Minister George Grenville, passed the American Revenue Act, otherwise known as the Sugar Act. The Sugar Act placed duties on goods imported into the colonies such as molasses, textiles, and wine. In the case of molasses, the new duty was lower than the one which had been in place; however, Grenville was determined that the duties imposed by the Sugar Act would actually be collected which had not been the case in the past. British customs officers began to enforce the duties aggressively. Bribery of customs officials and smuggling, which had previously been rampant, became increasingly difficult. The Sugar Act was certainly unpopular but eventually it gained grudging acceptance from the colonists.

The Stamp Act: In March 1765 Grenville and the British Parliament followed up the Sugar Act with the Stamp Act. The Stamp Act provided for direct taxation on printed items such as newspapers, pamphlets, and even playing cards. Unlike the Sugar Act the Stamp Act taxed domestically produced goods as well as goods imported from abroad. For example, a newspaper published in Boston was required to have the appropriate stamp, purchased from the local stamp agent, affixed to it prior to sale. Failure to follow this procedure was grounds for the publisher's prosecution by a British court.

The Stamp Act enraged the colonists. A member of the Virginia House of Burgesses, Patrick Henry, proclaimed that only they, the elected representatives of Virginia, had the right to tax the Virginia colonists. As the colonists had no voice as to who served in the British Parliament, they felt any taxes levied on them by Parliament were invalid. **"No taxation without representation"** became the battle cry of the day.

The Stamp Act inspired violence on the part of many colonists. The group known as the Sons of Liberty intimidated and attacked stamp agents and others working for the British. Bonfires fueled by stamp paper were lit from Boston to Charleston.

The Stamp Act Congress: In October 1765 nine colonies sent delegates to the Stamp Act Congress in New York. The delegates were united in their opposition to the Stamp Act and wanted to send Britain an official message expressing their displeasure. Pennsylvania delegate John Dickinson drafted the "Declaration of Rights and Grievances." Addressed to King George III, the document respectfully outlined the colonists' points of contention with the Stamp Act. Dickinson stressed that, although the colonists were unhappy with taxation without representation, they remained loyal subjects of the British Monarch.

The unrest in the colonies coupled with a colonial embargo on British made goods led Parliament and King George III to repeal the

Stamp Act in March 1766. Word of the repeal was greeted with celebration in the colonies. By the summer of 1766 tranquility had returned.

The Townshend Acts: The repeal of the Stamp Act left the British in the same financial pinch they had been in prior to the Stamp Act's implementation. Britain's equivalent to the modern-day U.S. Secretary of the Treasury, Chancellor of the Exchequer Charles Townshend, looked again to the colonies for additional tax revenue. In June 1767 the British Parliament passed the Townshend Acts. The Townshend Acts imposed additional duties on goods imported into the colonies such as glass, paper, and tea. Given that these were import tariffs and not direct taxes, such as those which had been imposed under the Stamp Act, Townshend and Parliament did not anticipate similar trouble. They were wrong.

The colonists responded to the new duties by drastically cutting back their consumption of imported goods. British goods were replaced by comparable goods produced within the colonies or done without completely. Colonial merchants who continued to carry British made goods were subject to harassment and attack.

To stem any possible violence arising from the Townshend Acts, the British increased their troop presence in the colonies. The presence of these troops angered the colonists further. Under the provisions of the Quartering Act, the colonists not only had to heed the demands of the British troops but were required to provide the troops with food and shelter as well.

The Boston Massacre: On March 5, 1770 the tension between the colonists and the British troops culminated with the Boston Massacre. What began as an incident of colonists taunting and throwing snowballs at a group of British soldiers ended with the soldiers discharging their muskets into the mob. Eleven colonists were shot. Five died. The incident created such hostility among the colonists that the British troops were forced to abandon Boston for their own safety. The Boston contingent of the British Army would spend the next four years stationed outside the city.

The summer of 1770 saw relative tranquility return to the colonies once again. The new British Prime Minister, Lord Frederick North, recognized that the Townshend Acts were not working and had them rescinded. Sensitive to the colonial anger over the Boston Massacre, the British troops assumed a low profile in the colonies. Again the focus of the typical colonist shifted from battling British tyranny to surviving everyday life.

Samuel Adams: The colonial furor created by the Stamp Act and the Townshend Acts aroused in certain men questions, not only regarding Britain's right to tax the colonies, but as to whether Britain had the right to govern the colonies at all. Among these men was Samuel Adams, the consummate American rabble-rouser. Sam Adams, the leader of the Boston Sons of Liberty, became committed to securing colonial independence from Britain. Many say that Adams was the true father of the American Revolution.

In 1773, three years after the rescission of the Townshend Acts, Adams grew concerned by the complacency he saw around himself. Adams wanted to find some way to step up the tension. He needed an issue, something to reignite the colonial fire. He found that issue in tea.

The Boston Tea Party: The summer of 1773 saw one of Britain's largest trading companies, the East India Company, in severe financial trouble. Not wanting to see the company go under, Prime Minister North issued the company a monopoly over the North American tea trade. The plan called for the company to sell its surplus tea directly to the colonists, avoiding the middlemen both in Britain and in the colonies. The colonists would have the opportunity to buy their tea at a discount and the company would get the cash infusion it so desperately needed.

Instead of being joyful at the prospect of inexpensive tea the colonists were upset by the British move. Colonial tea merchants were angry about being excluded from the transaction. Colonists everywhere were disturbed by what they perceived as undue British interference in colonial business affairs. In November 1773 East India ships were anchored in colonial harbors from Boston to Charleston, fully stocked with unsold tea.

The three tea ships in Boston Harbor offered Sam Adams the opportunity he was looking for to relight the colonial fire. On the night of December 16, 1773 Adams and his followers boarded the ships and dumped the tea leaves into Boston Harbor.

The Coercive Acts: Britain's response to the Boston Tea Party was one of outrage, just as Adams had expected and wanted. In the spring of 1774 the British Parliament passed the Coercive Acts, referred to as the Intolerable Acts in the colonies. The first act ordered the Boston port closed to all commercial traffic until restitution was made for the dumped tea. The second act removed the powers of the publicly elected Massachusetts Assembly, shifting all governmental responsibilities to the colony's royal appointees. Third, a new Quartering Act was put into place. Now the colonists not only had to pay for the room and board of the British troops, but they were also obligated to take individual soldiers into their own homes. Following the tea party British troops moved back into Boston itself.

The First Continental Congress: The Coercive Acts brought delegates from throughout the colonies to Philadelphia in September 1774. The delegates at the First Continental Congress met to discuss what was to be done about the Coercive Acts and to rally around Massachusetts. The delegates agreed to suspend all trading with Britain. They also agreed that Massachusetts should establish its own independent government and raise a militia. They demanded from Britain the immediate rescission of the Coercive Acts. Although revolution was on the minds of many who participated in the First Continental Congress, the body stopped short of endorsing such action.

Back in England King George III had no intention of rescinding the Coercive Acts. He increased Britain's military presence in the colonies, especially in Massachusetts, and prepared for war. As George III wrote in September 1774, "the colonies must either submit or triumph."

The Shot Heard 'Round the World: The Massachusetts colonists did arm themselves as prescribed by the Continental Congress. Back rooms became arsenals and colonists throughout New England prepared for battle. Having received word of a major colonial arsenal at Concord, Massachusetts, the commander of the British troops in Boston, General Thomas Gage, sent 700 of his men to seize the arsenal. In the late-night hours of April 18, 1775, the British troops began their march from Boston to Concord. The element of surprise the British hoped to achieve by moving at night was foiled when Paul Revere, William Dawes, and Samuel Prescott rode ahead of the British troops to warn their fellow colonists of the oncoming peril. At Lexington, midway between Boston and Concord, the British were met by 77 men from the Massachusetts militia. Inevitably the shooting began and soon the Battle of Lexington was over. When the smoke cleared eight colonists lay dead, and the British resumed their march to Concord.

By the time the British arrived in Concord, shortly after daybreak, the pre-warned villagers had relocated most of their munitions from the town's center to the surrounding countryside. The British discovered and disposed of only a small fraction of the munitions which had been in Concord the night before. By midday the weary British troops began their long march back to Boston. This was when the real fighting began. Hundreds of colonists lined the route from Concord to Boston and greeted the British troops with sniper fire. Having been on their feet since the previous night, the lethargic troops made easy targets. By the time their fateful march was over, the British had sustained over 250 casualties.

THE AMERICAN WAR OF INDEPENDENCE

Word of the Battles of Lexington and Concord spread quickly throughout the colonies. On May 10, 1775 colonial delegates met again in Philadelphia at the Second Continental Congress. The delegates made one last effort for peace, sending King George III the Olive Branch Petition which called for the repeal of the Coercive Acts and an immediate cessation of violence. Knowing their peace proposal would likely fall on deaf ears in Britain, which it did, the delegates also prepared for war. They appropriated funds for the establishment of the Continental Army. To reinforce the idea that this was not just New England's struggle, they decided that a Southerner, George Washington of Virginia, should lead the army. In June 1775 Washington set off for Boston.

The Siege of Boston: The Battles of Lexington and Concord marked the beginning of the siege of Boston. In May 1775 British Generals William Howe, Henry Clinton, and John Burgoyne joined General Gage in Boston to help lead the growing number of British troops. The British troops controlled Boston itself but the surrounding countryside was in the hands of the colonial rebels.

The Battle of Bunker Hill: In June 1775 colonial troops moved on Boston by securing and fortifying Breed's Hill. Breed's Hill gave the colonists a precipice from which they had a clear shot at the British position in the city. On June 17, 1775 the British moved to take the hill. 2,200 British troops commanded by General Howe staged a full-frontal attack on the colonists entrenched on Breed's. Short on ammunition, colonial commander William Prescott ordered his men, "Don't fire until you see the whites of their eyes!" The dug-in colonists let loose against the British with deadly accuracy. The Battle of Bunker Hill (named for an adjacent hill) was a British blood bath. The British sustained over 1,000 casualties, compared to just over 400 for the colonists. In the end the British took Breed's as the colonists were forced to retreat when they ran out of ammunition. Nevertheless, the battle was a great boost for the rebels.

The British Evacuate Boston: General George Washington arrived in Cambridge, Massachusetts to take charge of the ragtag group of New Englanders which became the Continental Army on July 3, 1775. Washington's men were short on ammunition and had no artillery. Fortunately for Washington, in May colonial forces led by Benedict Arnold and Ethan Allen had captured Fort Ticonderoga in upper New York from the British and confiscated its many heavy cannons. Unfortunately over 200 miles of nearly impassable terrain separated Ticonderoga from Boston. Yet with the help of some Yankee ingenuity, hearty oxen, and sturdy snow sleds, Washington received his cannons in January 1776. On March 4, 1776 Washington's men captured the high ground at Dorchester Heights, just south of Boston, and trained the Ticonderoga cannons on the British encampment below. Without a shot fired British General William Howe decided to evacuate. The last British troops set sail from Boston on March 17, 1776 never to return.

The Quest for Canada: While Washington and his troops laid siege to the British troops stationed in Boston, colonial forces under Benedict Arnold and Richard Montgomery set their sights on conquering the British in Canada. On November 13, 1775 Montgomery and his men captured Montreal. From there they sailed up the St. Lawrence River to join Arnold who was making plans to take the British fortification at Quebec. On New Year's Eve morning the colonists attacked Quebec in the midst of a furious snowstorm. The cold weary colonists were no match for the British. When the Battle of Quebec was over Montgomery lay dead and Arnold was forced to abandon Canada.

The Battle of Sullivan's Island: In early 1776 Britain looked to establish a military presence in the southern colonies. On the morning of June 28, 1776 British naval vessels commenced their bombardment of colonial Fort Moultrie on Sullivan's Island in Charleston Bay. Fort Moultrie's builder, Colonel William Moultrie, had used palmetto logs in the construction of the fort. Palmetto wood is known for its great pliancy and resiliency. Therefore the British cannonballs did not destroy the fort but rather bounced off the fort's palmetto walls. Protected, the colonial gunners wreaked havoc on the British ships. By nightfall each of the British ships had been damaged, one permanently. An attempt to land ground troops on Sullivan's Island earlier in the day had failed. Defeated, the British hoisted anchor and sailed off in the middle of the night.

The Declaration of Independence: As the war between Britain and the colonists heated up the pressure increased for the colonial leaders to sever all ties with the mother country. In January 1776 colonist Thomas Paine published and distributed his pamphlet, "Common Sense." "Common Sense" criticized the British government under King George III and presented the case for colonial independence. Paine was tremendously successful in arousing popular support for independence. Also supporting the case for independence was the fact that the colonial leaders were looking towards Britain's archenemies, France and Spain, for military and economic support. They knew their requests would be heeded more readily if France and Spain were certain that, in victory, the colonists would not return to the British Empire.

On July 4, 1776 the Continental Congress endorsed the Declaration of Independence. Drafted by Virginia delegate Thomas Jefferson, the document declared the colonies, "Free and Independent States" and "Absolved from all Allegiance to the British Crown." Thus, the conflict between Britain and the colonies officially became the American War of Independence.

The Loyalists: Word of the Declaration of Independence soon spread throughout the colonies. The news aroused jubilation in many colonists but there were those who greeted the news with great trepidation. A considerable number of colonists were dead set against separation from Britain. They considered themselves loyal British citizens and desired to remain subjects of King George III. These loyalists came in a variety of forms. Many kept their opinions to themselves for fear of angering their neighbors. Others actively fought their colonial brothers on behalf of the British Crown.

Defeat in New York: Once Washington had driven the British from Boston; he moved his forces to New York. Washington anticipated correctly that the British would attempt to invade New York to isolate the belligerent New Englanders from the rest of the colonies.

As expected the British began arriving in New York Harbor in July 1776. They secured Staten Island unopposed and made plans to attack Washington's men on Long Island. On August 27 British troops led by General William Howe attacked the colonial garrison at Brooklyn Heights on Long Island. Washington's army was outnumbered and outmaneuvered by the British. The war might have ended then had Howe not pulled his troops back from pursuing the retreating colonial troops. Remembering the slaughter on Breed's Hill, Howe wanted time to consider his next move carefully. Howe's hesitation gave Washington the time he needed to save his army. On the night of August 29 Washington and his men crossed the East River to Manhattan, abandoning Long Island.

On September 15, 1776 British troops and Hessians, German mercenaries fighting for the British, began landing on Manhattan. For the second time Washington found himself up against the wall. Outnumbered by the British and Hessian ground troops, Washington's men also had to contend with the British Navy which had surrounded Manhattan. Again the war might have been lost had the city of New York not caught fire in the early morning hours of September 21. The fire distracted the British and gave Washington time to evacuate Manhattan.

Of note, on September 22, 1776 the British executed one of Washington's men who had been caught spying on the British troops. The man's name was Nathan Hale, and he is remembered for the heroic words he was reported to proclaim as the noose was placed around his neck, "I only regret that I have but one life to lose for my country."

The New York campaign was disastrous for George Washington. Realizing his army was on the verge of extinction, Washington retreated across New Jersey and the Delaware River into Pennsylvania. The area which now constitutes the New York City metropolitan area was firmly in the hands of the British.

Victories at Trenton and Princeton: As the Christmas of 1776 approached the troops of the Continental Army were a sad lot as they camped in the Pennsylvania countryside. Convinced the Continental Army had ceased to be a threat, British commander Howe was content to spend Christmas in New York. Washington decided he needed to do something to bolster the morale of his troops and re-establish the Continental Army as a credible fighting force. He set his sights on the Hessian outpost at Trenton, New Jersey.

On Christmas Day night Washington and his men crossed the Delaware River. They reached the Hessian outpost in Trenton, New Jersey by daybreak. The 1,400 Hessians, groggy from the previous night's festivities, quickly surrendered to the Continental Army. The news of Trenton's fall shocked Howe. He dispatched General Charles Cornwallis and 5,500 of his best men to Trenton to defeat Washington once and for all. Not wanting to engage Cornwallis head-on, Washington quietly marched his men out of Trenton the night before Cornwallis arrived. On January 3, 1777 Washington attacked and captured the British post at Princeton at Cornwallis' rear flank. Princeton provided Washington's men with valuable supplies which would help sustain them through the remaining winter months. On January 6 Washington reached Morristown, New Jersey, where he established quarters for the remainder of the winter.

The Battles of Saratoga: In June 1777 General "Gentleman Johnny" Burgoyne and 8,000 British troops invaded New York from Canada. Burgoyne intended to capture the Hudson River Valley, thereby completing the separation of New England from the rest of the colonies. Burgoyne failed. Tired, short of supplies, and slowed by their unfamiliarity with the terrain, Burgoyne's troops were ill-prepared when they met colonial forces, led by Generals Horatio Gates and Benedict Arnold, at Freeman's Farm, New York on September 19, 1777. The First Battle of Saratoga was followed by the Second Battle of Saratoga on October 7, 1777. Both battles went badly for Burgoyne. Surrounded and outnumbered, Burgoyne surrendered on October 17, 1777.

The British Take Philadelphia: Unfortunately, Washington was not as successful as Arnold and Gates in the fall of 1777. In August General Howe and 15,000 British troops sailed up the Chesapeake Bay, disembarked, and began marching toward Philadelphia. Not wanting to lose the seat of the Continental Congress to the British, Washington rushed to head off Howe. In September 1777 the two armies collided on the banks of the Brandywine Creek, just to the southwest of Philadelphia. Soundly defeated, Washington was forced to retreat and the Continental Congress was forced to abandon Philadelphia which fell to the British on September 26, 1777. Washington's men set up camp at Valley Forge, Pennsylvania and prepared for the long, bitter winter ahead.

France Enters the War: In the summer of 1778 France entered the war against the British. French participation in the American War of Independence was brought about through the efforts of Benjamin Franklin who was serving as an envoy of the Continental Congress in Paris. Fearing a French naval blockade of the Delaware River, British General Henry Clinton, who had taken over William Howe's command, returned his troops to New York, ceding Philadelphia to Washington. With the British concentrated in New York, Washington relocated his headquarters from Pennsylvania to West Point, New York. Sporadic fighting would continue in the North through the end of the war but after 1778 the focus of the war would be in the South.

The Southern Campaign: In November 1778 British commander Clinton sent 3,500 troops sailing southward from New York. The British landed on the Georgia coast in December and captured the settlement of Savannah. Firmly entrenched in Georgia, the British staged several attacks on South Carolina during the summer of 1779. The attacks were successfully repulsed by the South Carolina militia led by Benjamin Lincoln.

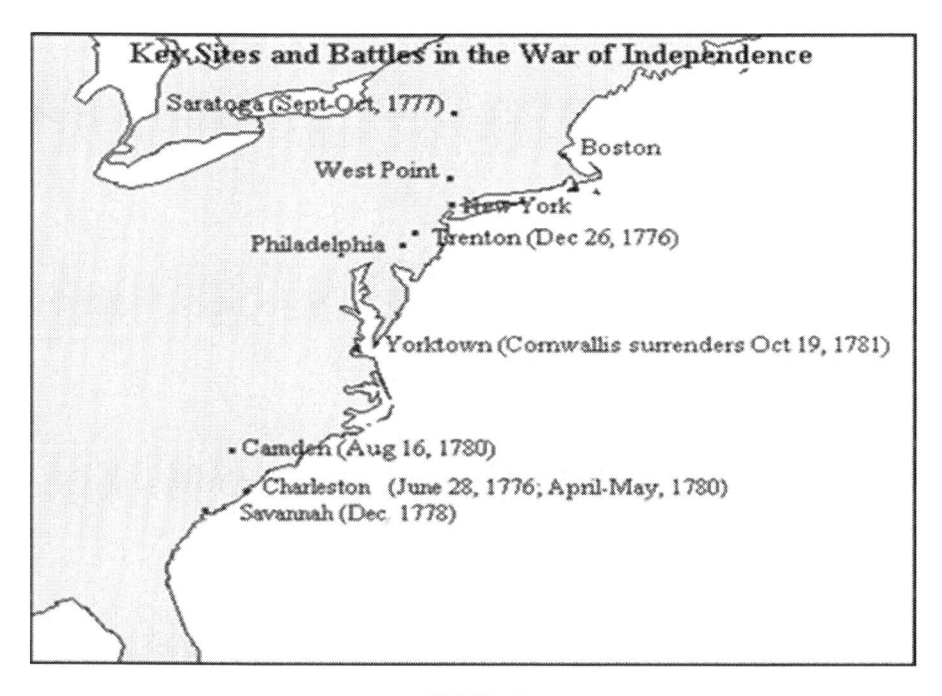

```
Key Sites and Battles in the War of Independence
   Saratoga (Sept-Oct, 1777).
                              Boston
        West Point .
                    . New York
   Philadelphia .* Trenton (Dec 26, 1776)

              Yorktown (Cornwallis surrenders Oct 19, 1781)

   . Camden (Aug 16, 1780)
    Charleston  (June 28, 1776; April-May, 1780)
    Savannah (Dec 1778)
```

Exhibit I

The Battle of Charleston: By the end of 1779 General Clinton became convinced that conquering the South was the best way to ensure a British victory in North America. In December Clinton and 10,000 of his men set sail from New York for Charleston, South Carolina. The British successfully landed troops both north and south of the city. On April 8, 1780, the British began to bombard the city. Cut off, Benjamin Lincoln was forced to surrender Charleston to the British on May 12, 1780.

After the fall of Charleston, Clinton returned to New York, content to leave the southern campaign to his second in command, General Charles Cornwallis. Cornwallis achieved another British victory in August at Camden, South Carolina, where he killed 900 colonial troops and captured over 1,000. Camden would prove to be the last major British victory of the war.

Benedict Arnold's Treachery: Meanwhile in New York, Benedict Arnold, hero of Saratoga and commandant of the colonial post at West Point, was preparing to turn West Point over to the British. Financially strapped, Arnold sold out to the enemy. Luckily, Arnold's plot was uncovered before he was able to secure West Point's surrender. Fearing for his hide, Arnold escaped from West Point in September 1780 and joined the British Army. Benedict Arnold, who had the potential to be remembered as one of the great American generals, is remembered instead as its most notorious traitor.

Guerrilla Warfare in the South: Following his victory at Camden, South Carolina, General Cornwallis came under ever increasing attacks from colonial hit and run squads. The commander of the southern colonial forces, General Nathaneal Greene, preferred guerrilla warfare to head-on confrontations with the British. Through the winter and spring of 1781, the British and the colonists engaged in several skirmishes in South Carolina, North Carolina, and Virginia. In August 1781, Cornwallis and his men retreated to the Yorktown Peninsula in Virginia to await supplies and reinforcements from the British Navy.

Surrender at Yorktown: A navy did arrive off the coast of Yorktown in August 1781. Unfortunately for Cornwallis, it was the French Navy. When British ships arrived in early September to resupply Cornwallis, the French drove them off. Blockaded by sea, Cornwallis was also sealed off by the colonists from any escape routes by land. Washington and his men rushed south to join the siege. Outnumbered, surrounded, and short on supplies, Cornwallis and his 8,000 men surrendered on October 19, 1781. The last major military confrontation of the war was over.

The Aftermath of Yorktown: The American War of Independence could have easily continued after Cornwallis' surrender at Yorktown. The surrender was indeed a blow to the British but they were far from defeated militarily. General Clinton and his men continued to have a firm grasp on New York; however, after Yorktown the will of the British to continue fighting was exhausted. What was once thought of as a minor insurrection had turned into a major war for the British. By late 1781 the British were not certain that victory in North America was possible. Even if they did finally win, many in Britain realized that governing a large group of disgruntled and rebellious colonists, halfway around the world, would prove to be a nightmare. Consequently, the British pushed for peace.

The Treaty of Paris: Representing the Continental Congress at the peace talks in Paris were John Jay, John Adams, and Benjamin Franklin. The Treaty of Paris was signed on September 3, 1783, officially ending the war. Under the terms of the treaty, the colonies collectively gained recognition as an independent nation which would be known as the United States of America. The new nation also received title from Britain to the territory between the Appalachian Mountains and the Mississippi River which Britain had won from France in the French and Indian War. Britain did retain its holdings in Canada. The Treaty of Paris was well received by the citizens of the newborn nation.

THE BIRTH OF A NATION

The 1776 Declaration of Independence marked the birth of a new nation. This birth brought a whole new host of questions to the forefront. What form of government would lead this new nation? Would this new entity take the form of one united nation or several independent nations? The resolution of these questions was made all the more urgent by the fact that the survival of the young nation hinged on its ability to defeat a European superpower in war.

The Continental Congress served as the federal government of the colonies (states) during the War of Independence. After independence was declared in the summer of 1776, it was decided that the role of the federal government should be defined more clearly. In March 1781 the Articles of Confederation were adopted.

The Articles of Confederation: The Articles of Confederation outlined the structure and role of the federal government. The federal government was to be run by the Congress, in which each of the states had one vote. The Congress had the right to vote on matters such as declaring war, negotiating treaties with other nations, and borrowing money. Yet Congress was not given the power to levy taxes, to regulate domestic or international trade, or to enforce its own laws. The Articles of Confederation, in fact, provided for a very weak federal government. This weakness was by design. The colonists feared that establishing a strong centralized government would bring back the same kind of tyranny, albeit in a different form, which they had experienced with the British.

The Articles of Confederation sufficed during the war. The largely autonomous states were united by the wrath they shared for a common enemy. Each state, more or less, did its part voluntarily to contribute to the war effort.

However, united in war, the states grew increasingly divided in peace. States became embroiled in border disputes with each other. They enacted tariffs on interstate trade which hindered commerce and resulted in post-war economic stagnation. The states quit contributing funds to the federal government. Unable to raise taxes on its own, Congress could not support its army. Also lacking a strong central government, the United States was unable to conduct effective foreign policy.

Shays' Rebellion: To pay off its war debts, Massachusetts implemented large increases in its property taxes following the war. These taxes were particularly hard on the state's many small farmers who were already being hurt by the weak economy. Those who were unable to pay their taxes and other debts faced the possibility of having their farms repossessed. These small farmers, many of whom had fought in the War of Independence, grew angry. They had not worked this hard and fought a war for the privilege of becoming homeless. In the autumn of 1786, the farmers began to organize. In January 1787 over 1,000 farmers led by army veteran Daniel Shays stormed the arsenal at Springfield, Massachusetts.

What could have developed into civil war in Massachusetts was easily squelched by the state militia. Those identified as leaders of the rebellion were tried, convicted, and then pardoned by a state legislature that had become sympathetic with their concerns. As a result of the rebellion, laws were changed to help alleviate the plight of the Massachusetts farmers.

More importantly, Shays' Rebellion caused Americans to begin thinking about law and order. Although the rebellion was successfully put down by the state militia, people questioned as to whether future rebellions in other states could be halted so easily. If civil war broke out in one state would it spread to neighboring states? Also, if the individual states had trouble keeping the peace locally, what chance would they have of warding off an attack from another nation such as Spain, France, or Britain?

The Constitutional Convention: Americans grew to realize that their survival depended upon establishing a stronger central government, one which could keep order and provide for the common defense. In May 1787 delegates from the states met in Philadelphia at the Constitutional Convention. Presided over by George Washington, the delegates assumed the monumental task of designing a new federal government.

The delegates met for four straight months, during which time they brainstormed, presented their ideas, argued, and compromised. Finally, on September 17, 1787, the delegates signed the final draft of the Constitution. The delegates, who had conducted their meetings with the utmost secrecy, were now ready to present the fruits of their labor to the American public.

The Constitution: The Constitution defined the duties and limitations of the new federal government. It provided for three branches of government: the **Executive**, the **Legislative**, and the **Judicial**. Each branch would operate independently and have certain checks on the powers granted to the other branches. For example only the Legislative branch would have the ability to pass laws, but the Executive branch could veto laws passed by the Legislative branch, and the Judicial branch could rule laws unconstitutional (an implied power). In turn, the Legislative branch would have the power to remove the head of the Executive branch, the President, or any judge in the Judicial branch through the power of impeachment. In the eyes of the architects of the Constitution, this system of ***checks and balances*** would prevent any one branch of the federal government from growing too powerful.

The Constitution also defined the relationship between the federal government and the states. Under the Articles of Confederation, each state had the right to regulate and tax interstate and foreign trade. The Constitution stipulated that these rights be taken away from the states and given to the new federal government. The states would also lose their right to print money. The states would retain most of their rights to regulate intrastate activities, provided their actions did not contradict the Constitution.

The Connecticut Compromise: In return for turning over many of their powers to the new federal government, the states would select who served in this government. A major point of controversy in the Constitutional Convention was the degree of representation each state would receive. The less populous states wanted each state to have equal representation. Predictably, the more populous states desired proportional representation based on population. The Connecticut Compromise addressed the concerns of both parties by providing for two bodies of Congress. In one, the House of Representatives, each state would be allotted seats based on population. For example, a state with five times the population of another would receive five times the number of congressional seats. In the other legislative body, the Senate, states would be allotted two seats each, regardless of population. The head of the Executive branch, the President, would be elected by the states with each state having the number of electoral votes equal to its total number of senators and representatives. Presidents would serve four-year terms. An indecisive Presidential election would result in the House of Representatives electing the President.

The Three-Fifths Compromise: Many of the northern delegates to the Constitutional Convention wanted to use the document to outlaw slavery throughout the states. The southern delegates made it clear that they would not be part of a Union in which the right of individuals to own slaves was abridged. Consequently, language was included in the Constitution which protected the property rights of slaveholders. As slaves constituted a substantial portion of the southern population, the southern delegates demanded that slaves be counted in the census for the purpose of awarding seats in the House of Representatives. The Northerners, arguing that the Southerners themselves considered slaves as property, believed slaves should not be counted. In the end, the two sides compromised, agreeing to count each slave as three-fifths of a person when determining the population of a given state for allotting House seats. Ironically and *disgustingly*, by their mere existence, southern slaves helped to bolster the political power of their owners, power their owners would use to ensure these slaves would remain slaves well into the future.

Suffrage Rights: The U.S. Constitution remained silent as to who would be allowed to participate in the electoral process, preferring to leave this issue to the individual states. As a result, white males, who dominated the state governments in the late 1780s, continued to extend the right of suffrage to their fellow white males. Black men would not be enfranchised with the vote until the latter half of the nineteenth century. Women, black or white, would not be guaranteed the right to vote until 1920.

The Amendment Process: The writers of the Constitution wisely realized that its survival would depend on its ability to adapt to the times. In particular, many **foresaw the day that slavery would need to be abolished once and for all throughout the Country**. That abolishment would need to become part of the Constitution. Consequently, a mechanism was outlined in Article V of the Constitution by which amendments could be made to the Constitution. The amendment process was **designed to be arduous in order to dissuade the passage of trivial amendments**. Yet if it became clear to the people of the United States that a change in the Constitution was necessary, that change could be made without discarding the entire document.

The Bill of Rights: One weakness of the U.S. Constitution was that it was largely silent on issues of individual rights and freedoms. The drafters of the Constitution intended originally for such issues to be left to the individual states. When the delegates to the Constitutional Convention went out to sell their document to the American public, it became clear the public wanted certain individual liberties guaranteed at the federal level.

In 1789 Virginian James Madison proposed twelve amendments to the Constitution. Of these, ten were ratified. These first ten amendments to the U.S. Constitution became known as the Bill of Rights. **The Bill of Rights is the cornerstone which would make the United States the premiere bastion and defender of liberty and freedom worldwide in the years to come.** The individual liberties guaranteed by the Bill of Rights are summarized as follows:

- *First Amendment: Freedom of religion, speech, and the press. Individuals have the right to assemble peaceably and to petition the government for a redress of grievances.*
- *Second Amendment: The right to bear arms.*
- *Third Amendment: Freedom from having troops quartered in one's home.*

- *Fourth Amendment: Freedom from unreasonable search and seizure.*
- *Fifth Amendment: The right not to be denied life, liberty, or property without due process of law. The right not to be tried twice for the same offense. Exempts individual from testifying against self.*
- *Sixth Amendment: The right to a speedy, public trial. The right to be informed of charges pending. The right to defense counsel and to call witnesses on one's behalf. The right to face accusers.*
- *Seventh Amendment: The right to trial by jury.*
- *Eighth Amendment: Freedom from cruel and unusual punishment.*
- *Ninth Amendment: Provides for individual rights not explicitly stated in the Constitution.*
- *Tenth Amendment: Powers not delegated to the federal government by the Constitution, nor prohibited by it to the states, are reserved for the states and the people.*

In June 1788 the Constitution was adopted as the law of the land. The Bill of Rights was added in 1791. Elections were held in early 1789. In April 1789 the newly elected representatives, senators, and the nation's first President, George Washington, took their places in the capital of the United States, New York City.

The Washington Years: President Washington had his work cut out for him when he assumed office on April 30, 1789. The concept for the new federal government, as outlined by the U.S. Constitution, had to be made reality, and it was Washington's responsibility to oversee this process. President Washington knew that to be successful he needed to surround himself with bright and ambitious men. Washington appointed New York lawyer John Jay as the first Chief Justice of the Supreme Court. He named Henry Knox as his Secretary of War. The two most prominent men in his administration were his Secretary of the Treasury, Alexander Hamilton, and his Secretary of State, Thomas Jefferson.

Alexander Hamilton: Alexander Hamilton was a proponent for a strong activist federal government. He believed that the government should play an active role in the national economy and in maintaining national order. Shortly after taking office, Hamilton proposed that the new federal government assume the debts of the old federal government. Without the power to tax, the Continental Congress had assumed considerable debt in order to finance its war expenditures. Hamilton believed this debt needed to be honored at face value in order to ensure the future credit of the United States of America. Additionally, Hamilton argued that the new federal government should assume the remaining war debts of the individual states, as these debts had been incurred for the "common good" of the nation.

The Bank of the United States: Hamilton also pushed for the creation of a centralized, government-run bank, the Bank of the United States. Hamilton believed that the establishment of a government-sponsored central bank was necessary to handle the receipt and disbursement of federal funds and to manage the nation's money supply. The Bank of the United States began operations in the summer of 1791.

Thomas Jefferson: In contrast to Hamilton, Jefferson firmly believed that a government governs best when it governs least. A Southerner, Jefferson was opposed to the federal government assuming the remaining war debts of the states, noting such a proposal would penalize the southern states which had been much more successful in paying down their war debts than their northern counterparts. Also, Jefferson opposed Hamilton's Bank of the United States, arguing the creation of such an institution went beyond the powers granted to the federal government by the U.S. Constitution. Eventually, Jefferson agreed to support Hamilton's debt proposals in return for Hamilton's support for locating the permanent seat of the U.S. federal government in the South. Consequently, Hamilton's proposals were passed into law, and the District of Columbia, an area carved out of the southern states of Maryland and Virginia, became the permanent site for the nation's capital.

Hamilton vs. Jefferson: The rivalry between Jefferson and Hamilton was heightened when France and Britain went to war in 1793. The 1789 French Revolution had resulted in the deposition and decapitation of French King Louis XVI. The new revolutionary government declared war on Britain on February 1, 1793, thereby launching the fifth Anglo-French war of the eighteenth century. Given the United States' experience with Britain and the fact that the French people, like the Americans, had had the fortitude to overthrow their oppressive monarch, Jefferson supported the French in the war. Ever the pragmatist, Hamilton supported the British in the war, noting that Britain was a more important trading partner to the U.S. Not wanting to be dragged into this conflict, Washington decided that the nation should remain neutral. Washington eventually succumbed to Hamilton's desires and in 1795 presented Jay's Treaty to the American people. Negotiated with the British by envoy John Jay, Jay's Treaty fell short of proclaiming U.S. support for the British in the war but was nonetheless construed by the American public as being pro-British.

The Rise of Political Parties: Jefferson, who left the Washington Administration in December 1793, began to attract support for his pro-France small government beliefs. Supporters of Jefferson became known as Democratic-Republicans. In 1795 the Democratic-Republicans used the unpopular Jay's Treaty as a platform to attack the policies of Hamilton and Washington. The Democratic-Republican Party gained widespread public support, especially in the South. Supporters of Hamilton and Washington, who were known as Federalists, continued to maintain their power base in the Northeast. The rivalry between the Democratic-Republicans and the Federalists grew ever more heated and bitter in the mid and late 1790s.

The 1796 Election: As the 1796 Presidential election approached, Washington found himself fed up with the growing political factionalism and bickering. He decided against seeking a third term in office. The 1796 Presidential election pitted Democratic-Republican Thomas Jefferson against John Adams, who was serving as Washington's Vice President. Adams narrowly won.

John Adams and the Sedition Act: John Adams, who was a younger cousin of Samuel Adams, was not the most popular of Presidents. In the latter half of his administration, Adams came under severe attack and criticism from his Democratic-Republican opponents. Armed with a Federalist Congress, Adams signed the Sedition Act into law in 1798. The Sedition Act enabled Adams to imprison those individuals who spoke out against him. Adams used the Sedition Act to jail several of his critics, including Democratic-Republican newspaperman Benjamin Franklin Bache who was the grandson of the deceased, but eternally loved, Benjamin Franklin.

The Sedition Act left the Democratic-Republicans and the nation aghast. The Sedition Act clearly violated the First Amendment's provisions for free speech and free press and was therefore unconstitutional; however, the Judicial branch, dominated by Federalists, refused to rule it as such. Luckily, the 1800 Presidential election was fast approaching. By passing and enforcing the Sedition Act, Adams had disaffected many in the voting population who considered him to be an enemy of liberty. The election of 1800 made clear exactly how the public felt about the government infringing on its right to speak freely.

1800-1860: THE NATION GROWS

The period from 1800 to 1860 was one of tremendous growth for the United States. The land area of the nation tripled during this period as the U.S. grew from being an eastern seaboard nation to one which stretched from "sea to shining sea." The population of the nation increased from 5.3 million in 1800 to 31.4 million in 1860. This increase was due to internal propagation, European immigration, and involuntary African immigration (i.e., the slave trade). As the nation's population increased the number of Americans living in the nation's largest cities skyrocketed. In 1800 roughly 60,000 people lived in the nation's largest city, New York. By 1860 the population of New York City was over 800,000. The number of Americans living west of the Appalachian Mountains increased dramatically. Western cities such as Cincinnati, Chicago, Saint Louis, and San Francisco sprouted during the early and mid-1800s.

The focus of the northern economy shifted from agriculture to manufacturing in the early and mid-nineteenth century. Industries such as coal mining, textile manufacturing, and railroad equipment manufacturing became prominent in the North. On the other hand, agriculture continued to dominate the southern economy. Cotton production, in particular, rose to prominence such that by 1860 cotton was by far the leading export of the United States. Cotton ensured that the South would remain heavily dependent on slave labor up until the time of the U.S. Civil War. In turn, this southern dependence on slavery would increase the tensions between white Southerners and their northern neighbors, most of whom had given up slavery within their own states by the turn of the century and would look upon southern slavery with ever-increasing skepticism and disgust as the nineteenth century progressed. A delicate political balance between proslavery (southern) and antislavery (northern) forces would be maintained up until 1850. In 1850 this balance would be disrupted, resulting in an eruption of North-South tensions which would culminate with the U.S. Civil War.

The Election of 1800: The 1800 Presidential election resulted in a first-place tie between two Democratic-Republicans, Virginian Thomas Jefferson and New Yorker Aaron Burr. Incumbent John Adams finished third. Prior to 1804 the constitution had not made a distinction between electoral votes cast for the intended President (in this case Jefferson) and the intended Vice President (in this case Burr). This constitutional issue would be addressed by the Twelfth Amendment, ratified in 1804. As it was provided for by the original U.S. Constitution, the selection of the nation's chief executive became the responsibility of the House of Representatives. The House chose Thomas Jefferson.

The Jefferson Administration: Jefferson assumed office on March 4, 1801 in the nation's new capital, Washington D.C. He was joined by a Democratic-Republican Congress as the Federalists had sustained heavy damage in the 1800 elections. From the beginning Jefferson worked to scale down government and send the message that the federal government was the servant, rather than the master, of the people. Jefferson cut taxes and spending. He let the despised Sedition Act expire when it came up for renewal in the summer of 1801.

The Louisiana Purchase: The highlight of the Jefferson Presidency came in 1803 with the Louisiana Purchase. In 1800 Spain, which had controlled the Louisiana Territory since the end of the French and

Indian War, was coerced into ceding the Louisiana Territory to France. French Emperor Napoleon Bonaparte had intended to re-establish a French presence in North America; however, by 1803 Bonaparte found himself preoccupied with his European conquests. In January 1803 Jefferson sent envoy James Monroe to Paris with instructions to offer Bonaparte $2 million for a small plot of French-controlled territory at the mouth of the Mississippi River. Bonaparte, who had given up on his plan to conquer North America, offered to sell the entire Louisiana Territory to the United States for a sum of $15 million. Monroe agreed.

When Monroe returned with news of the purchase, President Jefferson was surprised and ecstatic. The Louisiana Purchase doubled the land area of the United States. It offered a seemingly limitless supply of virgin land for future American pioneers. In August 1803, Jefferson sent Meriwether Lewis and William Clark to explore the new territory for the government. The Louisiana Purchase was widely regarded as a great prize and ensured Jefferson's reelection in 1804.

Jefferson's Foreign Policy Crisis: Jefferson's second term did not go as smoothly as his first. Once again France and Britain were at war when Jefferson began his second term. French Emperor Napoleon Bonaparte, who had risen to power from the ashes of the French Revolution, became resolute in his desire to conquer all of Europe. The British were equally resolute to ensure that Napoleon would not succeed. Both warring parties wanted the support of the United States and neither would accept U.S. neutrality. When the U.S. failed to take sides, wanting instead to conduct business as usual, U.S. ships, sailing in international waters, became subject to seizure by both nations. The British went one step further by *impressing* able-bodied U.S. sailors into service with the Royal Navy.

In June 1807 the *U.S.S. Chesapeake* was stopped by the *H.M.S. Leopold* of the British Navy just off the coast of Virginia. U.S. Navy Commodore James Barron rejected the British order to allow his ship to be searched for impressment candidates. The British ship fired on the *Chesapeake*, disabling her, and impressed four of her sailors.

The Embargo Act: The attack on the *U.S.S Chesapeake* enraged Jefferson and the American public. In December 1807 Jefferson pushed the Embargo Act through Congress. Essentially the Embargo Act banned all foreign trade. Jefferson wanted the seizures and impressments to stop and he became convinced that keeping U.S. ships at home was the only way to accomplish this. Jefferson also wanted to punish France and Britain, both of whom shared profitable trade relationships with the United States.

The embargo was a disaster. By 1808 the U.S. economy had grown highly dependent on foreign trade. Southerners exported a good portion of their agricultural output to Europe. Northerners built and manned the ships which served as the vehicles of trade. The Embargo Act left both in the cold and plunged the nation into a deep economic depression. Public protest and open defiance of the embargo became rampant. On March 1, 1809 Jefferson, who had decided against seeking a third term in office, repealed the Embargo Act. Three days later he left office.

James Madison: Jefferson's successor, Democratic-Republican James Madison, inherited Jefferson's foreign policy problems when he took office on March 4, 1809. Madison resumed trade with both France and Britain; however, he stipulated that once one party formally revoked its policy of interfering with American shipping, the embargo would be reinstated on the other party if it did not soon follow suit. This was Madison's way of coercing both France and Britain into respecting the sovereignty of American shipping.

Seeing an opportunity to strike at his opponent Napoleon offered to recognize American maritime sovereignty in August 1810. Madison received word of this in November and used it to step up pressure on the British. With no response from Britain Madison declared an embargo on U.S.-British trade in March 1811.

The U.S. embargo was hard felt by the British. On June 16, 1812 the British agreed to respect American maritime rights in return for the resumption of U.S.-British trade. Unaware of this, the U.S. Congress declared war on Britain on June 18, 1812. By the time word of the British capitulation reached Washington D.C., the second war with Britain was well underway.

The War of 1812: There is no single clear-cut reason why the U.S. declared war on Britain in the summer of 1812. Britain's disrespect of U.S. maritime sovereignty combined with her despised practice of impressing U.S. sailors were indeed slaps in the young nation's face. Yet these factors alone were not enough to convince most Americans for the need for a second war with Britain. What pushed the U.S. into the war were the war hawks in Congress. War hawks, such as Congressmen Henry Clay of Kentucky and John C. Calhoun of South Carolina, were convinced that war with Britain would achieve beneficial results for the young nation. The war hawks blamed the British for increased Indian unrest on the frontier. By waging war with Britain, they hoped to undermine British support of the Indians. Additionally, the war hawks believed that through war the U.S. could make territorial gains at the expense of British held Canada. The fact that the U.S. was unprepared for an all-out war against the British in the summer of 1812 did not seem to matter. By June 1812 these Congressional war hawks, who were extremely talented politicians, were able to convince enough of their fellow politicians that starting a second war with Britain was actually a good idea.

The 1812 Canadian Campaign: In the summer of 1812 a plan was devised for a three-pronged attack on Canada. American forces would attack the British from Detroit, Niagara Falls, and Lake Champlain. The hope was to catch the British off guard.

The Canadian Campaign of 1812 was disastrous. The Detroit force, led by General William Hull, invaded Canada in July 1812 but returned to Detroit when Hull got cold feet. The British followed Hull's force back to Detroit, surrounded his position, and forced his surrender. Defeat for the Americans at Niagara Falls was assured when the second and third waves of the American invasion force refused to cross the Niagara River, separating the U.S. and Canada. The brave but naive men of the first wave, who did cross the river, were swallowed up by the British troops on the other side. Finally, the planned attack on Canada from Lake Champlain failed to materialize due to widespread reticence among the U.S. troops.

Of note, the U.S. Navy fared a little better in 1812 achieving a few minor victories over the British Navy. The men of the *U.S.S. Constitution* served their country particularly well, destroying the British frigates, *Guerriere* and *Java*. The *Constitution's* valiance and durability in the service of her country during the war would earn her the nickname "*Old Ironsides*" and a permanent berth in Boston Harbor.

U.S. Victories: The war improved for the Americans in 1813. In September 1813 the U.S. Navy scored a substantial victory over its British counterpart on Lake Erie. The U.S. victory at the Battle of Lake Erie gave the Americans control of the lake and caused the U.S. commander, Oliver Hazard Perry, to issue his famous proclamation,

"We have met the enemy and they are ours." In October the Americans scored a second victory, this time on land, at the Battle of the Thames in Canada. American forces led by General William Henry Harrison soundly defeated a combined force of British and Indian soldiers.

In April 1814, the French Emperor Napoleon Bonaparte was deposed, bringing an end to the European war. Bonaparte's demise enabled the British to focus exclusively on their war in North America.

The British Take Washington: The British attempted to shift the focus of the American military away from the Canadian border by attacking the seat of the federal government, Washington D.C. In August 1814 an expedition of 4,000 British troops sailed up the Chesapeake Bay toward the capital. Madison and Congress were forced to flee Washington which fell to the British on August 24, 1814. The British proceeded to burn down the White House, the Capitol, and several other government buildings. Leaving the city ravaged, the British proceeded to Baltimore where they staged an attack on the American forces at Fort McHenry. Of note, the intense British artillery attack on Baltimore inspired one American, Francis Scott Key, to compose the *Star-Spangled Banner.* Unable to dislodge the Fort McHenry defenders, the British sailed out of Chesapeake Bay in October.

On December 24, 1814 American and British peace negotiators, meeting in Europe, signed the Treaty of Ghent, ending the war. The treaty called for an immediate cessation of hostilities and the restoration of the U.S.-Canadian border to what it was before the war.

The Battle of New Orleans: As news traveled only as fast as the fastest ship in 1814, the greatest U.S. victory of the war was achieved two weeks after it was officially over. On January 8, 1815 British troops, who had landed at the mouth of the Mississippi River in late December, staged a full-frontal assault on entrenched American forces at New Orleans, Louisiana. At the Battle of New Orleans, U.S. forces led by Andrew Jackson inflicted over 2,000 British casualties while sustaining fewer than 100 themselves. Although meaningless as it was from a strategic perspective, the Battle of New Orleans helped to bolster American pride and would propel Andrew Jackson to the newly rebuilt White House fourteen years later.

The Monroe Administration: Madison's successor, fellow Democratic-Republican James Monroe, assumed office on March 4, 1817. During Monroe's Presidency the Americans signed two treaties with the British. One demilitarized the U.S.-Canadian border. The other established the 49th parallel as the northern boundary between the Louisiana Territory and Canada. In 1819 Monroe's Secretary of State, John Quincy Adams, negotiated the purchase of Florida from Spain.

The Missouri Compromise: By 1819 the tension between the northern free states and the southern slave states had heated up considerably. Southern politicians were under ever increasing pressure to protect their "peculiar institution" from the meddling of the Northerners. In 1819 the northern free states, given their larger populations, enjoyed a majority in the House of Representatives. Yet since there were 11 free states and 11 slave states in 1819, the Southerners were able to block antislavery legislation in the Senate in which each state enjoyed equal representation regardless of population. When the territory of Missouri petitioned Congress to enter the Union as a slave state in February 1819, the free state dominated House granted statehood, conditional on Missouri providing for the gradual emancipation of its slaves. The southern senators balked at the House bill, arguing that Missouri would eventually become a free state, thereby eliminating the slave state-free state balance in the U.S. Senate.

Congress was at an impasse. The impasse was resolved when the people of Maine petitioned Congress to enter the Union as a free state. The Missouri Compromise of 1820 maintained the Senate balance by offering Missouri admission to the Union as a slave state and granting Maine admission as a free state. Additionally, as a concession to the North an amendment was added to the Missouri Compromise which prohibited slavery in the Louisiana Territory outside of Missouri, north of the 36-30' parallel. A potential crisis was averted, temporarily.

The Monroe Doctrine: The domination of the European powers, most notably Spain, over their Central and South American colonies diminished greatly in the early nineteenth century. As Europe was busy contending with Napoleon Bonaparte, Latin revolutionaries seized upon this opportunity to declare independence from European control. Given their own revolutionary heritage, Americans strongly sympathized with their Central and South American counterparts. By the early 1820s Europe, having recovered somewhat from Napoleon's escapades, began to look at the possibility of re-establishing its influence in Latin America.

In December 1823 the President issued the Monroe Doctrine. The Monroe Doctrine proclaimed the United States to be the protector of the Western Hemisphere. The doctrine stated that the Americas would no longer be subject to any future European colonization attempts. Monroe recognized the presence of those European nations which had retained control of their American possessions but forbade any European power from trying to reassert control where control had been lost. Monroe also recognized the legitimacy of many new Latin American revolutionary governments.

Although the United States did not have the military might to enforce the Monroe Doctrine when it was issued in 1823, it did send a strong message to the European superpowers regarding U.S. resolve on this issue. The Monroe Doctrine has remained a basic tenet of U.S. foreign policy up to the present day.

The Election of 1824: The election of 1824 marked the end of the Democratic-Republican Party as a united entity. Unable to find a single palatable candidate, the Democratic-Republicans split into different factions, each centered around the person they felt should be the next President. **The party supporting Andrew Jackson, the Democratic Party, would last to the present day.** The other factions quickly dissipated after the election. When the election of 1824 was over, Andrew Jackson, the hero of New Orleans, had won pluralities in both the popular and electoral votes. Yet as the 1824 vote was split between several candidates, Jackson was unable to garner a majority of the electoral vote. As provided for by the Constitution, the responsibility for selecting the sixth President of the United States was shifted to the House of Representatives. The House selected John Quincy Adams, Monroe's Secretary of State and the son of the second President of the United States.

John Quincy Adams: The Presidency of John Quincy Adams was cursed from the start. Jackson's supporters cried foul over the selection of Adams as President. The elections of 1824 and 1826 resulted in a Congress which was increasingly pro-Jackson. Adams' ability to get any substantive legislation through Congress was quite limited. Finally in 1828 Adams lost to the man who many Americans felt should have been President four years earlier.

Andrew Jackson: On March 4, 1829 Andrew Jackson was inaugurated the seventh President of the United States. Jackson enjoyed widespread grassroots popularity. Reared modestly, Jackson rose up to achieve status as a military leader and a successful businessman. To many, Jackson was the embodiment of the American dream. Upon reaching the nation's top office, Jackson did not forget who he was or where he came from. He saw himself as representing the common man and used his position to lash out at the people and the institutions of the "eastern aristocracy."

The Bank War: Jackson saw Hamilton's Bank of the United States as a symbol for all he despised. In his eyes, the national bank served the interests of the wealthy at the expense of the common man. In 1832 Jackson vetoed the bill to renew the bank's charter. He withdrew federal funds from the bank, forcing the bank, in turn, to call in its loans to individuals and businesses. The fall of the Bank of the United States precipitated a fiscal crisis which resulted in an economic depression. Luckily for Jackson, the full effects of the depression were not felt until after he left office in 1837.

Indian Removal: Andrew Jackson is also remembered for his abysmal treatment of the Indians. As a soldier, Jackson established himself as an effective Indian fighter. As President, Jackson continued what had become a lifelong quest to dispose of the North American Indian. In 1830 Jackson signed the Indian Removal Act into law. This act authorized the relocation of all remaining eastern Indian communities to lands west of the Mississippi River.

In 1832 the Cherokee Indians of Georgia contested that state's plan to seize their land all the way to the Supreme Court. In the case of *Worchester v. Georgia*, the Supreme Court, led by Chief Justice John Marshall, found in favor of the Cherokees, ruling the State of Georgia's actions as unconstitutional. Nevertheless, Jackson, committed as he was to Indian removal, refused to abide by the Supreme Court's ruling. Jackson is reported to have said about the Supreme Court Chief Justice, "John Marshall has made his decision, now let him enforce it." The removal of the Cherokees and all the other eastern Indian communities was continued as planned.

Martin Van Buren: A protégé of Andrew Jackson, Martin Van Buren, succeeded him as President in 1837. During Van Buren's Administration, the nation underwent a severe economic depression, largely attributable to Jackson's dismantling of the Bank of the United States. Also, during Van Buren's Administration, Jackson's plan to remove all Indians to locations west of the Mississippi River was nearly completed. By 1838 the forced removal of the eastern Indians from their homelands, the so-called *Trail of Tears*, was in full swing. By 1840 the Indian population had been effectively removed from the eastern half of the United States.

William Henry Harrison and John Tyler: As a result of the poor economy, Van Buren lost his 1840 bid for reelection. On March 4, 1841 the Whig Party and William Henry Harrison gained control of the White House. Formed during the Presidency of Andrew Jackson, the Whig Party attracted members from every level of society who shared a common sentiment. They hated Jackson.

Harrison's Presidency was short lived. Harrison fell ill on his inauguration day. One month later he died of pneumonia. Harrison's Vice President, John Tyler, served the remainder of Harrison's term in office. Not trusted within his own party, Tyler was not nominated by the Whigs in 1844.

The Polk Administration: Tennessean James Polk returned the Presidency to the Democrats in March 1845. An ardent expansionist, Polk was tremendously successful in growing the land area of the United States. In 1846 Polk signed a treaty with the

British over the disputed Oregon Territory. Before 1846 both the U.S. and Britain laid claim to the Oregon Territory. Under the 1846 treaty this dispute over ownership was resolved, with the two parties agreeing to divide the Oregon Territory at the 49th parallel, thereby establishing the 49th parallel as the U.S.-Canadian border from the Lake of the Woods to the waters of the Pacific Ocean. Additionally, by waging war against Mexico in 1846 and 1847, Polk was able to secure for his nation the lands which currently make up the southwestern United States.

Texas and the Build-up to the Mexican War: In the early 1820s American pioneers led by Stephen Austin began settling in Texas which was then part of Mexico. Mexico, which had gained its independence from Spain in 1821, welcomed these early settlers. However, with the ascension of Antonio Lopez de Santa Anna to the top post in the Mexican government, conditions for all Mexicans worsened. In 1834 Santa Anna disbanded the Mexican Congress and established himself as supreme dictator. Not wanting to be subject to Santa Anna's tyranny and wary of Mexico's antislavery stance, Texas seceded in December 1835.

The Alamo: Santa Anna was quick to move against the rebellious Texans. In February 1836, Santa Anna and several thousand of his men laid siege to a force of about 200 rebellious Texans who were defending the Alamo in San Antonio. The siege lasted thirteen days, concluding when Santa Anna's men were finally able to overwhelm the stoic Alamo defenders on March 6, 1836.

The Texas Republic: On April 21, 1836 Santa Anna met his match at San Jacinto, Texas. Santa Anna's army was routed by a much smaller Texan force led by Sam Houston. Captured, Santa Anna was forced to sign a treaty recognizing Texan independence. The Texas Republic was established, and Sam Houston was elected its president. Knowing they faced an uphill battle as an independent state, Texans overwhelmingly supported a referendum to seek annexation of their state into the United States in 1836. The U.S. Congress, torn by whether Texas should enter the Union as slave or free territory, would not move to annex Texas until 1845.

In 1845 Congress finally annexed Texas. The annexation came over the protests of the Mexican government which still viewed Texas as a rebellious Mexican province. In May 1845 President Polk ordered General Zachary Taylor to the Texas-Mexican border to dissuade any attempts on the part of Mexico to reoccupy Texas.

Polk Proposes a Sale: James Polk's strong expansionist rhetoric was a decisive factor in his 1844 election win. Once elected, Polk was determined to make good on his word. After the Texas annexation, Polk made overtures to the Mexicans about purchasing what is now the southwestern United States. Insulted and angered, the Mexicans rebuked Polk.

The Mexican-American War: Polk grew anxious for war against Mexico so that he might achieve militarily what he could not achieve peacefully. Yet Polk knew that an unprovoked U.S. attack on its Mexican neighbor would be bad for public relations. Luckily for Polk, on April 25, 1846, Mexican troops crossed the Rio Grande and attacked a small detachment of Zachary Taylor's army, inflicting sixteen U.S. casualties. The attack itself was militarily insignificant but it gave Polk the provocation he needed to declare war on Mexico.

The Mexican-American War was short lived and a rout for the U.S. In the autumn of 1846, General Taylor and his men pressed southward into Mexico from the Texas border. In the spring of 1847, U.S. forces led by General Winfield Scott launched an amphibious assault on the southern Mexican city of Veracruz. After numerous skirmishes Scott and his men reached the Mexican capital, Mexico City, in September 1847, bringing an end to the war.

In February 1848 U.S. and Mexican officials signed the Treaty of Guadalupe Hidalgo, officially ending the Mexican-American War. Under the terms of the treaty, Mexico ceded Texas, California and the land in between to the United States. In return the U.S. agreed to pay Mexico $15 million. Polk got what he wanted.

Taylor and Fillmore: President Polk decided against seeking a second term in 1848. Capitalizing on the absence of a strong Democrat candidate, the Whigs nominated General Zachary Taylor to be their candidate for President. On November 7, 1848 Taylor was elected the twelfth President of the United States.

California: In late 1848 word reached the East that gold had been discovered in the newly acquired California Territory. News of the discovery started a wave of westward migration. In 1849, thousands of "forty-niners" journeyed to California in search of the elusive metal. California's non-Indian population, which had been about 5,000 before the discovery of gold, swelled to over 100,000 by the end of 1849.

In December 1849 California applied for admission to the Union as a free state. President Taylor pushed for unconditional and immediate admission but was met with strenuous opposition from the southern politicians. As was the case with Missouri in 1820, the admission of California would have the effect of upsetting the slave state-free state balance in the U.S. Senate.

The Compromise of 1850: In January 1850 Senator Henry Clay from Kentucky put forth a series of resolutions which he felt would address the concerns of both North and South with regards to the granting of statehood to California. Clay's resolutions laid the foundation for the Compromise of 1850 which gained the support of Congress. The Compromise of 1850 enabled California to enter the Union as a free state, but, in turn, made several concessions to the South, including the enacting of a strong fugitive slave law which required the northern free states to return escaped slaves to their southern owners.

President Taylor, however, did not see the need for compromise. He saw no reason for conditions being placed on California's admission to the Union. It seemed certain that the Compromise of 1850 would attract the Presidential veto. Yet Taylor would never get the chance. On July 4, 1850 Taylor became ill. After five days of aggressive and misguided doctoring Zachary Taylor died. In September 1850 Taylor's successor, Millard Fillmore, signed the Compromise of 1850 into law.

Pierce and Buchanan: In 1852 Democrat Franklin Pierce was elected the fourteenth President of the United States. In 1856 he was replaced by fellow Democrat James Buchanan. The Presidencies of both men came at a time when the Union was gripped by dissension over the question of slavery. Neither man was equipped with the skills or the passion needed to resolve the brewing crisis.

THE ROOTS OF CIVIL WAR

The underlying cause of the U.S. Civil War was slavery. Slavery was present throughout both the North and the South at the time of the War of Independence. However, in the late eighteenth and early nineteenth centuries slavery was gradually abolished in the northern states. As slavery had never achieved the status of indispensability in the northern economy, it was not difficult for the early antislavery activists in the North to arouse popular opposition to this unnecessary evil.

On the other hand, in the South slavery remained an integral part of the economy and the overall way of life up until the time of the Civil War. The smooth running of the plantations, which dominated the agrarian economy of the South, depended on the availability of an inexpensive reliable labor force. In the mid-nineteenth century, most southern whites simply saw no alternative to slavery.

The Rise of Abolitionism: The United States was founded on the principle, as stated in Thomas Jefferson's Declaration of Independence, that "all men are created equal." To most Americans in the Revolutionary War era this short phrase served as a symbol of hope and national pride as they fought to free themselves from British rule. After the war many Americans found it difficult to reconcile this stated national principle with the fact that a substantial portion of the U.S. population was trapped in the institution of lifetime bondage known as slavery.

The first to call for slavery's abolishment were the Pennsylvania Quakers. The normally passive Quakers were uncharacteristically fierce as they spoke out against slavery which they found reprehensible. In 1775 the first American abolitionist society was founded in Philadelphia and counted Benjamin Franklin among its early members. Pennsylvania took the lead in the abolitionist movement, passing legislation in 1780 providing for the gradual emancipation of all its slaves. By the turn of the century, slavery had either been outlawed or was in the process of being outlawed in each of the northern states.

William Lloyd Garrison: With the North free abolitionists turned their attention to the South. In the 1830s northern newspaperman William Lloyd Garrison established himself as the chief spokesperson of the abolitionist movement. Garrison's newspaper, the *Liberator*, called for the immediate emancipation of all southern slaves. Garrison attacked slavery and the slaveholders with tremendous fervor. One of the most radical voices of his day, Garrison attracted supporters and enemies alike. Particularly among southern slave owners, Garrison's words aroused contempt and fear.

Frederick Douglass: Another prominent abolitionist was ex-slave, Frederick Douglass. Douglass, who had escaped to the North in 1838, was asked to speak about his experiences at a Boston abolitionist meeting in 1841. The self-educated Douglass enthralled the audience with his oratory skill and his passion. Thereafter Douglass received invitations to speak at abolitionist meetings throughout the North. Douglass wrote a best-selling autobiography in 1845 and began publishing his own abolitionist newspaper in 1848.

Harriet Beecher Stowe: Perhaps the greatest weapon in the abolitionist arsenal was a book, *Uncle Tom's Cabin*, published in 1852. Written by Harriet Beecher Stowe, *Uncle Tom's Cabin* illustrated vividly the disgusting and inhumane aspects of slavery. A bestseller, Stowe's novel brought additional support and credence to the abolitionist movement.

Although loud and visible, true abolitionists remained a small minority of the northern population. Most Northerners in the 1850s were against the spread of slavery. Yet for the sake of maintaining national peace, few Northerners were in favor of denying outright their fellow countrymen in the South their "peculiar institution."

Southerners React to the Abolitionists: Despite their minority status in the North the abolitionists were successful in inspiring fear in their white southern neighbors. The Southerners feared that as the abolitionists gained ever greater political power, they would eventually pressure the federal government into outlawing slavery nationwide. As early as the 1810s the Southerners had detected an antislavery lean in the northern dominated U.S. House of Representatives. Yet up until 1850 the Southerners had retained a sufficient number of seats to block antislavery legislation in the Senate. With California's admission to the Union as a free state in 1850 the southern senators found themselves in the minority and consequently could no longer guarantee the defeat of antislavery legislation.

The Fugitive Slave Law: In return for southern support for admitting California to the Union as a free state Fin 1850 the northern politicians agreed to the passage of a strong fugitive slave law. The Fugitive Slave Law of 1850 provided financial incentives to northern law enforcement officials for returning runaway slaves to the South. Slave catchers throughout the North were given free rein. The fugitive slave law inspired widespread anger among Northerners, many of whom viewed it as an extension of slavery to the North.

The Underground Railroad: Northern opposition to the fugitive slave law resulted in severe enforcement problems. Slave catchers in the North were subject to harassment and attack. Fugitive slaves jailed in the North were broken out before they could be returned to the South. Networks of safehouses developed from the southernmost free states to British controlled Canada where slavery was illegal. Collectively known as the Underground Railroad, these networks shuttled thousands of fugitive slaves to freedom.

The Kansas-Nebraska Act: By 1854 the southern politicians were extremely angry over the ineffectiveness of the fugitive slave law. Under the Compromise of 1850, they had agreed to admit California to the Union as a free state in return for what they now perceived as a worthless law. In January 1854 Senator Stephen Douglas, from the free state of Illinois, submitted a bill to Congress which he hoped would calm his southern colleagues. Douglas's bill, the Kansas-Nebraska Act, would provide the citizens of the newly settled Kansas and Nebraska Territories the opportunity to decide for themselves whether or not to allow slavery. Douglas believed such an act would be popular among the Southerners as it at least opened up the option for the spread of slavery. Douglas also believed that in the end his fellow Northerners would be satisfied as he predicted the settlers of Kansas and Nebraska would vote to ban slavery within their respective territories.

With the help of President Franklin Pierce, Douglas persuaded enough of his fellow Democrats to make the Kansas-Nebraska Act law. However, Douglas underestimated the furor which would arise in the North as a result of the act's passage. The Kansas-Nebraska Act invalidated the 1820 Missouri Compromise which had banned slavery in the western territory north of the 36-30' parallel. Many northern abolitionists denounced the Kansas-Nebraska Act as a conspiracy to spread slavery throughout the West. Kansas, itself, became an intensifier of tensions as proslavery and antislavery settlers began killing each other.

The Dred Scott Case: Further contributing to the tensions between proslavery and antislavery forces was the 1857 Dred Scott Case. Dred Scott, a slave, sued for his freedom on the basis that for five years he had lived with his owner in free territory. The Supreme Court, led by Chief Justice Roger Taney from the slave state of Maryland, ruled against Scott. Commenting on behalf of the court, Taney noted that, as a slave, Scott did not have the right to sue his owner in federal court. Additionally, Taney argued that as Scott was his *master's* property, Scott's *master* was constitutionally protected from having his property confiscated.

Taney's ruling essentially legalized slavery throughout the United States. According to Taney, slaveholders were protected by the U.S. Constitution from having their property (slaves) taken away. Since the property rights provisions of the Constitution applied equally to each of the states, the implication of Taney's ruling was that those states which had banned slavery within their own boundaries had violated the Constitution. Taney stopped short of calling for the repeal of the northern antislavery laws which would have been the logical next step. Nevertheless, his ruling enraged the North.

John Brown: Undoubtedly the Kansas-Nebraska Act and the Dred Scott decision helped to push one man, abolitionist John Brown, over the edge. In October 1859 Brown and his abolitionist posse captured the federal arsenal at Harper's Ferry, Virginia. Brown hoped that by raiding the arsenal and distributing the arms to local slaves he would spark a nationwide slave revolt. Brown's plan failed. A contingent of the Federal Army rushed to Harper's Ferry in late October and crushed his small force. On December 2, 1859, John Brown was dispatched to the gallows.

Although John Brown failed in his attempt to launch a slave revolt, he was successful in elevating the fears of many southern white people. The fear of a widespread slave revolt had always been present in the southern white community. Brown's actions brought this old fear to the forefront. The incident at Harper's Ferry convinced many in the South that creating a southern nation, separate from the North with all its John Brown, William Lloyd Garrison, and Frederick Douglass type individuals, was the only way to protect their way of life.

The Republican Party: In March 1854 the Republican Party was born with its first official meeting taking place in Ripon, Wisconsin. Republicans were united by their opposition to the spread of slavery and soon established themselves as the **main opposition to the proslavery Democratic Party.** Most were for the eventual abolition of slavery nationwide, but they realized they would have to take one step at a time. The Republicans gained considerable support in the North when Congress passed the unpopular Kansas-Nebraska Act. The Republicans received considerably more support after the *dreadful and despicable* 1857 Dred Scott decision.

In the aftermath of the Civil War, Republicans in Congress would push for Civil Rights for the newly freed slaves in the South through the Reconstruction Period. Unfortunately, down the road the Democrats would prevail, bringing **Congressional Republican Reconstruction** and the accompanying early Civil Rights movement in the South to an end in 1876.

Abraham Lincoln: In 1858 one man rose to the forefront of the Republican Party. In accordance with his party's doctrine, Abraham Lincoln was against the spread of slavery in the growing United States. Accordingly, Lincoln spoke out against both the Kansas-Nebraska Act and the Dred Scott decision. Yet Lincoln's primary conviction was that no matter what happened with the issue of slavery, the nation had to remain united.

The 1860 Election and Secession: On November 6, 1860 Republican Abraham Lincoln was elected the sixteenth President of the United States. To Southerners, Lincoln's election as President was unacceptable. After the election, the southern states began declaring their independence from the Union. On December 20, 1860 South Carolina seceded from the United States. In January 1861 Mississippi, Florida, Alabama, Georgia, and Louisiana followed suit. Thus, the Confederate States of America was born. Delegates from these states met on February 4 in Montgomery, Alabama to establish a Confederate government and a Confederate Army. Mississippian Jefferson Davis was elected the first and only president of the Confederacy. The early members of the Confederacy were joined later by Texas, Virginia, Arkansas, North Carolina, and Tennessee. In May 1861 Richmond, Virginia was designated as the capital of the Confederacy.

West Virginia: Of note, the citizens of northwestern Virginia balked at secession. When Virginia seceded from the Union in April 1861, they, in turn, seceded from the state of Virginia. In 1863 West Virginia entered the Union as an independent state.

THE AMERICAN CIVIL WAR

Four months passed between Lincoln's election and his inauguration on March 4, 1861. Lame Duck President James Buchanan did nothing to address the crisis which was gripping the nation. Upon taking office, Lincoln seemed uncertain as to what steps he should take to save the crumbling Union. Lincoln was hesitant about striking a first blow at the rebellious southern states.

Fort Sumter: In the winter of 1861, the Confederate states began seizing the federal facilities within their boundaries. Forts and arsenals were seized with little or no resistance from the federal officials in charge. On April 11, 1861, Confederate forces led by General P.G.T. Beauregard demanded the immediate surrender of the U.S. troops stationed at Fort Sumter in Charleston, South Carolina. The fort's commander, Major Robert Anderson, refused. On April 12, 1861 Beauregard began shelling Sumter. On the next day Major Anderson surrendered.

The shelling of Sumter gave Lincoln the provocation he needed to mobilize the North for war. Enraged by the Confederate aggression, Northerners enlisted in the Union Army in droves. The Southerners similarly mobilized. During the spring and summer of 1861, two great armies took shape, preparing to battle each other to the death.

The First Battle of Bull Run: In the summer of 1861, 22,000 Confederate troops under General Beauregard gathered at Manassas, Virginia, 25 miles southwest of Washington D.C. Fearing the Confederates were planning an invasion of the capital, Lincoln sent General Irvin McDowell and 28,000 Union Army troops to drive

Beauregard out of northern Virginia. On July 21, 1861, the two armies collided. An additional 9,000 troops under Confederate General Joseph E. Johnston joined the fray. The First Battle of Bull Run began well for the Union troops as they battered Beauregard's left flank. Yet Beauregard's left flank held, mainly through the efforts of General Thomas Jackson, who would earn the nickname "Stonewall" for his efforts that day. The tide of the battle turned when Beauregard sent Johnston's fresh reinforcements on a massive counterattack against the Union forces. Undertrained and undisciplined, the Union soldiers panicked at the sight of the charging Confederates. A mad, disorganized retreat followed. Washington D.C. might have fallen had the Confederates pursued the retreating Union Army. The Confederates did not pursue.

The disastrous Battle of Bull Run shattered in many a northern mind the concept that crushing the southern rebellion would be a quick, easy affair. Lincoln replaced Irvin McDowell with General George McClellan who spent the remainder of 1861 trying to shape up the Union Army so that the chaotic behavior exhibited by the Union troops at Bull Run would not be repeated.

The Western Campaigns of 1862: Realizing that putting down the southern insurrection would not be as easy as he once thought, Lincoln began making plans for an all-out war in the fall of 1861. A crucial part of Lincoln's plan to defeat the Confederacy was to attack the Confederate States from the West and gain control of the Mississippi River. In February 1862 Union forces led by General Ulysses S. Grant captured Fort Henry and Fort Donelson in northwest Tennessee. On April 6 Grant and his men engaged Confederate forces under General A.S. Johnston at Pittsburg Landing, Tennessee. The battle pitted 62,000 Union troops against 40,000 for the Confederacy. The two-day Battle of Shiloh resulted in 13,000 Union casualties and 11,000 Confederate casualties. By far the bloodiest battle to be fought in North America up to that point in history, Shiloh would soon be surpassed by bigger bloodier Civil War battles. In the end the Union persevered, and the Confederates were forced to retreat from western Tennessee.

While Grant was mopping up in Tennessee Union forces led by Admiral David Farragut launched an amphibious assault on New Orleans. In the spring and summer of 1862 New Orleans and Baton Rouge fell to Farragut, giving the Union control of the southernmost part of the Mississippi River.

The Peninsular Campaign: In the East Union commander McClellan drilled his troops from August 1861 to March 1862, in and around Washington D.C. Frustrated by McClellan's hesitance to deploy his troops in battle, Lincoln ordered McClellan to march on the Confederate capital at Richmond, Virginia. In April McClellan and his men landed on the Yorktown Peninsula in Virginia. It was not until June 1862 that McClellan and his 125,000 men approached the outskirts of Richmond. Consistently overestimating the troop strength of his opponent, McClellan hesitated repeatedly to attack the Confederates. McClellan's hesitation enabled Confederate General Robert E. Lee to deploy his much smaller force, which was guarding Richmond, in a series of hit and run attacks on the Union forces. Had McClellan consolidated his forces and launched an all-out attack on Richmond, the Confederate capital would have likely fallen and the Civil War might have come to an early conclusion. However such brash and bold leadership was simply not part of McClellan's personality. In July 1862 the Union troops returned to Washington D.C., abandoning their quest for Richmond. Many Union troops left wondering why they had journeyed to southern Virginia in the first place.

The Second Battle of Bull Run: McClellan was sidelined after his failed Peninsular Campaign. Union General John Pope faced the Confederates at Manassas, Virginia in August 1862. Pope was handily defeated by Confederate forces led by Stonewall Jackson, James Longstreet, and Robert E. Lee at the Second Battle of Bull Run. Pope retreated to Washington. President Lincoln, frustrated by his inability to find an effective military leader in the East, again turned to George McClellan.

The Battle of Antietam: Meanwhile Confederate General Lee went on the offensive, crossing the Potomac River and establishing a position in Maryland. Lee's objective was the Union rail center at Harrisburg, Pennsylvania. On September 17, 1862, McClellan's army met Lee's army at Sharpsburg, Maryland. The Battle of Antietam was essentially a draw, with both sides sustaining heavy casualties (over 26,000 combined). McClellan was successful in causing Lee to abandon his position north of the Potomac and return to Virginia. McClellan ordered his battered forces not to pursue the retreating Confederates.

The Battle of Fredericksburg: McClellan's failure to pursue Lee in the aftermath of Antietam angered Lincoln, and McClellan was relieved of his command. Lincoln wanted desperately to find a bold aggressive man to lead his army in the East. Lincoln's choice to replace McClellan, General Ambrose Burnside, would prove that aggressiveness alone does not make a good general. In November 1862 Burnside began moving his troops south toward Richmond. On December 13, 1862 Burnside's 120,000 men launched a head-on assault on Lee's 80,000 men, entrenched at Fredericksburg, Virginia, 50 miles north of Richmond. Poorly planned, Burnside's assault on the Confederates resulted in 13,000 Union casualties, compared to 5,000 for the South. Burnside's march to the Confederate capital was stopped in its tracks.

The Emancipation Proclamation: In September 1862 Abraham Lincoln issued the Emancipation Proclamation to the American public, calling for the freeing of slaves in Confederate controlled territory by January 1, 1863. Prior to issuing the proclamation, Lincoln had worried about the effects such a move would have on the northern war effort. Willing to fight and die to preserve the Union, most Northerners were unwilling to go to such lengths to abolish slavery. Subsequent to his proclamation, Lincoln took great pains to reinforce the idea that the Civil War remained first and foremost a struggle to preserve the United States of America. Abolishing slavery was of secondary importance.

Of note, the Emancipation Proclamation did not free those slaves held in slave states which had remained loyal to the Union. Lincoln did not want to alienate the slave owners of Missouri, Kentucky, Maryland, and Delaware by taking away their property. Regardless by the end of the Civil War the inevitable was made clear to all. Slavery in North America was dead.

By issuing the Emancipation Proclamation, Lincoln accomplished several things. For many, he raised the stakes of the Civil War to a higher moral plane. The proclamation opened up the Union Army for free black men. Blacks, who had a special interest in seeing the Confederacy fall, would serve with distinction in the Union Army through the remainder of the war. Finally, Lincoln's proclamation eliminated the threat that any European superpower would enter the war on the side of the Confederacy. Given that the abolitionist movement had spread successfully throughout Europe in the eighteenth and early nineteenth centuries, it was politically infeasible in 1863 for any European superpower to enter a war for the overt purpose of preserving slavery.

Key Battles of the U.S. Civil War

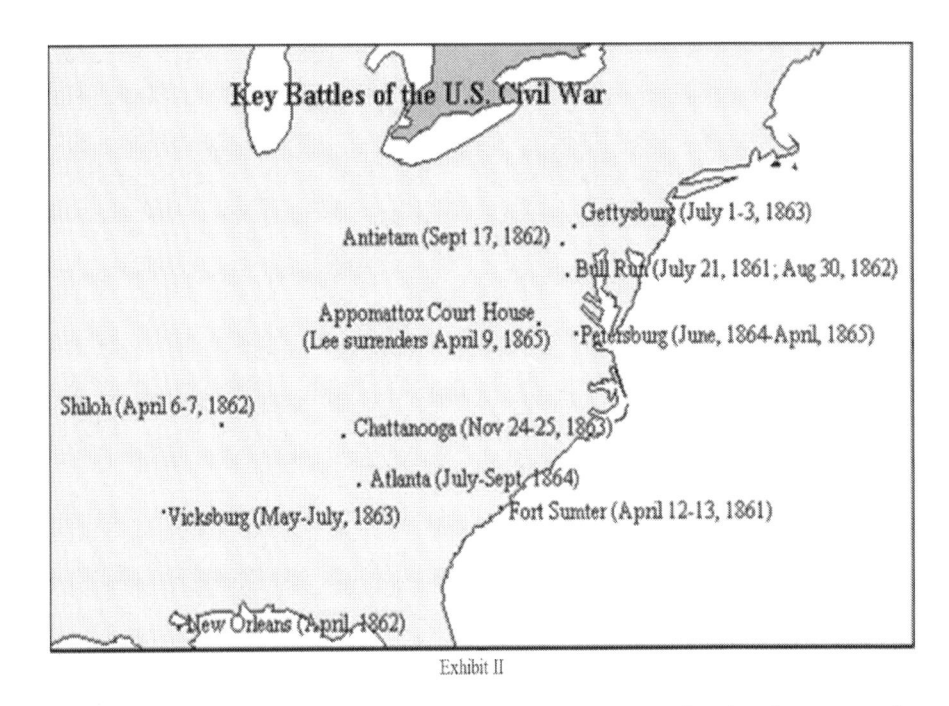

- Gettysburg (July 1-3, 1863)
- Antietam (Sept 17, 1862)
- Bull Run (July 21, 1861; Aug 30, 1862)
- Appomattox Court House (Lee surrenders April 9, 1865)
- Petersburg (June, 1864-April, 1865)
- Shiloh (April 6-7, 1862)
- Chattanooga (Nov 24-25, 1863)
- Atlanta (July-Sept, 1864)
- Vicksburg (May-July, 1863)
- Fort Sumter (April 12-13, 1861)
- New Orleans (April, 1862)

Exhibit II

The Siege of Vicksburg: In contrast to the quagmire in the East, the Union Army continued to make gains in the West. In early 1863 General Grant began planning for the capture of Vicksburg, Mississippi. The capture of Vicksburg would place the entire Mississippi River in Union hands. In May Grant captured Jackson, Mississippi, cutting off Vicksburg's main supply line. Then Grant surrounded Vicksburg. Unable to penetrate the city's formidable defenses, Grant was content to shell and starve the city into submission. On July 4, 1863 the 30,000 Confederate troops at Vicksburg surrendered unconditionally. The capture of Vicksburg placed the entire Mississippi River under Union control and cut off Louisiana, Arkansas, and Texas from the rest of the Confederacy.

The Battle of Chattanooga: From Vicksburg, Grant traveled to Chattanooga, Tennessee where his colleague General William Rosecrans had been in a yearlong bloody struggle for control of eastern Tennessee with Confederate General Braxton Bragg. Grant assumed the command of the Union troops at Chattanooga in October 1863. On November 24 Grant sent his men against Bragg's troops entrenched on Lookout Mountain, just outside the city. The following day the two armies battled on nearby Missionary Ridge. The two-day Battle of Chattanooga ended with Grant capturing Bragg's positions. Bragg and his men were forced to retreat to Georgia.

The Battle of Gettysburg: In the East Burnside's defeat at Fredericksburg was followed by another costly Union defeat at Chancellorsville, ten miles to the west, in May 1863. Pressing his advantage Robert E. Lee moved his troops north, invading Maryland and Pennsylvania in June. Lee hoped that by bringing the horror of war to the North he would shake up the Northerners who, in turn, would pressure President Lincoln into making peace with the Confederacy. On July 1, 1863 Lee's men engaged Union troops at Gettysburg, Pennsylvania. The first day of the three-day battle went well for the Confederates as they outnumbered the Union troops. Lee's men captured Gettysburg, forcing the Union troops to take up a defensive position just south of the town.

Large numbers of Union reinforcements began to arrive at Gettysburg on the evening of July 1. By the following morning, 85,000 Union troops under the charge of General George Meade faced Lee's 75,000 men. On the second day, Lee's men focused their attack on Meade's left flank. Some of the fiercest fighting of the day took place on a hill, Little Round Top, where Colonel Joshua Chamberlain and his men of the 20th Maine Regiment repulsed the charging Confederates. The second day of battle ended with the Union lines intact. On the third day, Lee made one last bold attempt to dislodge Meade's men, entrenched on the aptly named Cemetery

Ridge. The full-frontal assault known as Pickett's Charge resulted in thousands of casualties, disproportionately Confederate. Unable to dislodge Meade and with over a third of his force killed or wounded, Lee decided to withdraw his men from Gettysburg and Pennsylvania. The Battle of Gettysburg remains the bloodiest single battle ever fought on the North American continent. The Union suffered 23,000 casualties, and the Confederacy suffered 28,000 casualties. Gettysburg was the fatal blow for the Confederacy, even though the Confederate Army would struggle on for another two years.

Lincoln's Gettysburg Address: On November 19, 1863 Lincoln traveled to Gettysburg, Pennsylvania to pay tribute to the men who had fallen there so recently. Lincoln's short speech to the assembled crowd, the Gettysburg Address, is among the most remembered and revered speeches in American history.

Fourscore and seven years ago our fathers brought forth on this continent a new nation conceived in liberty and dedicated to the proposition that all men are created equal. Now we are engaged in a great civil war testing whether that nation, or any nation so conceived and so dedicated, can long endure. We are met on a great battlefield of that war. We have come to dedicate a portion of that field as a final resting-place for those who here gave their lives that that nation might live. It is altogether fitting and proper that we should do this. But, in a larger sense, we cannot dedicate, we cannot consecrate, we cannot hallow this ground. The brave men, living and dead, who struggled here have consecrated it far above our poor power to add or detract. The world will little note nor long remember what we say here, but it can never forget what they did here. It is for us the living, rather, to be dedicated here to the unfinished work which they who fought here have thus far so nobly advanced. It is rather for us to be here dedicated to the great task remaining before us-that from these honored dead we take increased devotion to that cause for which they gave the last full measure of devotion-that we here highly resolve that these dead shall not have died in vain, that this nation under God shall have a new birth of freedom, and that government of the people, by the people, for the people, shall not perish from the earth.   *Abraham Lincoln*

Sherman's March to the Sea: A protégé of Grant, General William Tecumseh Sherman, moved his troops from Chattanooga to Georgia in the spring of 1864. For most of the spring and summer, Confederate forces, led by General Joe Johnston and later General John Hood, kept Sherman's superior force bogged down in the northwest corner of the state. Finally, in September 1864 Sherman captured Atlanta. The fall of Atlanta opened all of Georgia for Sherman and his men. Sherman's subsequent "march to the sea" resulted in the complete destruction of northern Georgia. In December Sherman reached Savannah, Georgia on the coast and prepared for his 1865 march through South Carolina.

Grant's Virginia Campaign: Grant's numerous victories in the West convinced Lincoln to name him Supreme Commander of the Union Army. In May 1864 General Grant led 120,000 men against Lee's army of 65,000 in Virginia. Waging a war of attrition, Grant suffered over 55,000 casualties in several battles fought with Lee's forces in May and June. Union bloodletting became so great that many of Grant's men began pinning their names and addresses to their backs before going into battle so that their corpses could be identified more easily. Lee's losses were about 33,000 during this same period; however, unlike Grant, Lee did not have new troops joining his ranks to replace the fallen. By the summer of 1864, the South had lost nearly an entire generation of young men to death or crippling injury.

Surrender at Appomattox: In June 1864 Grant moved on to Petersburg, the Confederate rail transportation center of Virginia. Capturing Petersburg would cut off Richmond's major supply line and force the surrender of the Confederate capital. In response Lee's army rushed to defend Petersburg before Grant could stage an all-out attack on the city. Unable to take Petersburg by force, Grant was content to lay siege to Lee's forces defending the city. The siege of Petersburg lasted until April 1865, when Lee, realizing his army was dying, finally pulled out. Lee's men were unable to shake Grant's men who pursued them as they retreated from Petersburg. Realizing the game was up, Lee capitulated. On April 9, 1865 at Appomattox Court House, Lee surrendered his army to Grant, effectively bringing an end to the American Civil War.

Why the North Won the Civil War: The Union prevailed in the Civil War for one simple reason. The Union possessed greater resources than the Confederacy, in terms of both **material and manpower**. At the onset of the Civil War, the North possessed over 80% of the nation's manufacturing capacity and 70% of the nation's railways. In addition, the North controlled the nation's shipping which it used to blockade the South by sea. Most importantly, the North enjoyed a population advantage; 22 million people compared to the South's 9 million, of whom 3.5 million were black slaves. This translated into the North's having roughly 4.0 million men between the ages of 15 and 40 to draw upon for military service. The South had only 1.1 million white men in this age group, and this number dropped precipitously during the course of the war.

The Cost of the Civil War: By the end of the Civil War, over 600,000 Union and Confederate troops had lost their lives, comprising 2% of the nation's population. The war was particularly hard on the South. A large proportion of the young white men, who had left their homes to fight for the Confederacy, never returned. Many returned without arms or legs. Much of the South itself was in ruins after the war, as most military operations had been conducted on southern soil.

Lincoln's Assassination: On April 14, 1865, five days after Lee's surrender at Appomattox, Abraham Lincoln was shot while watching a play at Ford's Theater in Washington D.C. He died the following day. Consequently, the responsibility for healing the war-torn nation would fall to Lincoln's Vice President, Andrew Johnson.

1865-1900

The period from 1865 to 1900 was a boon for the industrial North. The North emerged from the Civil War stronger than ever. Men such as steelmaker Andrew Carnegie, oil magnate John D. Rockefeller, and financier J.P. Morgan led a private sector based post-war expansion which would result in the United States becoming an economic superpower by 1900. Best exemplifying the nation's economic growth were the railroads. In 1860 there were about 30,000 miles of track, concentrated mainly in the Northeast and Middle West regions of the nation. By 1900, over 200,000 miles of railroad track had been laid, spanning the entire nation.

Progress, however, had a price. Millions of northern men, women, and children worked up to 80 hours a week in hot, dangerous factories for meager wages. Newly arrived immigrants found themselves huddled in the slums of New York, Boston, and Chicago. Able to secure only the most wretched jobs, many immigrants realized that the American Dream was not to improve their own lives, but rather to work for better lives for their children and grandchildren. Corruption abounded on all levels of society. The nation's large corporations understood that, in order to conduct business effectively, the political pump needed to be primed. Bribery of government officials reached epidemic levels in the latter half of the nineteenth century.

By modern standards, most of the nation's population lived in abject poverty in the late nineteenth century. As a result, many of the nation's downtrodden workers turned to labor unions to improve their wages and working conditions. Countless unions came and went during the period from 1865 to 1900. Strikes and worker revolts were widespread but largely ineffective. Employers were tremendously successful in breaking strikes and busting unions. If all else failed, an employer could simply replace a disgruntled workforce with the next boatload of immigrants arriving from Europe. The nation's politicians, who viewed the unions as impediments to economic progress and saw that supporting big business could be financially quite lucrative, consistently sided with the large corporations against the unions. On several occasions, police and federal troops were employed to break strikes.

In contrast to the North, the South was in economic shreds following the Civil War. The Southerners went to work rebuilding their agrarian economy. Replacing the South's large slave plantations were numerous sharecropping farms. A typical sharecropping farm employed numerous ex-slaves to work the land. Poor and landless, southern blacks found themselves forced into the sharecropping system. Sharecropping offered most ex-slaves an existence which was little better than what they had known under slavery.

Reconstruction: Following the war both President Andrew Johnson and Congress realized that the federal government would have to play an active role in rebuilding the South; however, they disagreed tremendously over exactly how the federal government should proceed with this task.

Johnson desired to get the ex-Confederate states back into the Union as soon as possible following the war. He also wanted to be as lenient as possible in dealing with the ex-leaders of the Confederacy. Under the terms of the Thirteenth Amendment, ratified in December 1865, slavery was abolished throughout the nation. Nevertheless, Johnson remained silent as to what rights should be extended to the newly freed southern blacks. Johnson preferred to leave the issue of black rights to the individual states.

The Republican dominated Congress attacked Johnson's plan for being too lenient on the ex-Confederates. Also, the Republican Congressmen noted that the southern whites, left to their own devices, were doing everything in their power to keep the newly freed southern blacks subjugated. Establishing and enforcing key civil rights for southern blacks became a priority for Congress.

Congressional Reconstruction: As the year 1866 progressed, Congress wrestled the reigns of Reconstruction away from Johnson. In April 1866, Congress passed the Civil Rights Act which extended the rights of U.S. citizenship to the nation's blacks. The Civil Rights Act of 1866 gave the federal government the right to supersede the authority of state and local governments should they move to abridge the rights of their black citizens. Johnson vetoed the bill; however, Congress was able to muster the two-thirds vote necessary to override Johnson's veto, and the Civil Rights Act of 1866 became law.

In the summer of 1866 Congress drafted the Fourteenth Amendment. The Fourteenth Amendment was designed to make black civil rights a permanent part of the U.S. Constitution. The provisional governments of the ex-Confederate states were allowed to vote on the Fourteenth Amendment in late 1866. Each, except for Tennessee, rejected the Amendment. Consequently, Congress dissolved the provisional governments of each ex-Confederate state, except for Tennessee. In March 1867, Congress passed the Reconstruction Acts which required the ex-Confederate states to enfranchise their black citizens politically and to ratify the Fourteenth Amendment before being allowed back into the Union.

The Reconstruction Acts also prohibited many ex-leaders of the Confederacy from voting or holding state office. Finally, in 1869 Congress drafted the Fifteenth Amendment, which was formally ratified in 1870. The Fifteenth Amendment extended the right to vote to the nation's black men.

The Reconstruction Governments: The ex-Confederate states met the requirements of Congressional Reconstruction and re-entered the Union from 1868 to 1870. Running the new southern state governments were the newly enfranchised blacks, Northerners who had moved south after the Civil War (carpetbaggers), and southern whites who had remained politically enfranchised and chose to work within the boundaries of Congressional Reconstruction to rebuild their states. For the first time in American history, southern blacks were politically enfranchised.

Johnson's Impeachment: By enacting its own Reconstruction plan, Congress acted in defiance of Johnson who consistently vetoed Congressional Reconstruction legislation. Johnson's vetoes were overridden by Congress. By 1867 Johnson was an effectively powerless chief executive. In early 1868 the U.S. House moved to impeach Johnson, whom they viewed as being uncooperative and a nuisance. The Senate voted narrowly against backing up the House impeachment action.

Ulysses S. Grant: Although Johnson survived his 1868 impeachment trial, he was too tarnished and too ineffective to have any hope of winning the 1868 Presidential election. The 1868 Presidential election pitted Democrat Horatio Seymour against Republican and Civil War hero Ulysses S. Grant. On March 4, 1869, U.S. Grant was inaugurated the eighteenth President of the United States.

The Decline of Reconstruction: Grant had supported the strong Reconstruction measures passed by Congress during the Johnson

Administration. With the President and the Congress working together, many had high hopes for southern Reconstruction during the Grant Administration. Yet Grant proved unsuccessful in stemming a growing white backlash against Congressional Reconstruction in the South. The late 1860s gave rise to southern white supremacist groups such as the Ku Klux Klan and the Knights of the White Camellia. White supremacists terrorized blacks and did everything in their power to undermine their newfound political power. Grant's efforts to counter the tactics of these terrorist groups met with limited lasting success. Additionally, in 1872 the General Amnesty Act was passed which re-enfranchised thousands of southern whites who had been banned from voting and holding office due to their past service to the Confederacy. Now white supremacists could work both inside and outside the system to attack the black political power base.

Rutherford B. Hayes and the End of Reconstruction: The 1876 Presidential election between Democrat Samuel Tilden and Republican Rutherford B. Hayes marked the end of Reconstruction. The election itself produced no clear winner, as the results in three states were disputed. The Democrats and Republicans reached a compromise, whereby the Democrats would agree to support a Hayes Presidency if the Republicans agreed to pull the last of the federal army troops out of the South. Hayes became the nineteenth President of the United States and the federal army, which had served as the enforcement arm of Congressional Reconstruction, was removed from the South. Without the federal army watching over them, certain southern whites were free to undo much of what had been accomplished under Congressional Reconstruction. By 1878 most of the political and civil rights gains, achieved by southern blacks under Congressional Reconstruction, had been wiped away.

Custer's Defeat at Little Bighorn: Following the Civil War, the federal government turned its attention to the last remaining nomadic Indian tribes living in the western United States. On June 25, 1876, U.S. Army Lieutenant Colonel George Custer and his men met a force of Sioux warriors near the Little Bighorn River in southern Montana. The Battle of Little Bighorn was a rout for the Sioux. Custer and 260 of his men were slaughtered.

Little Bighorn propelled Sioux Chiefs Sitting Bull and Crazy Horse to legendary status; however, it was a costly victory for the Indian resistance movement in the West. Following Custer's demise, the resolve of European-Americans to destroy the last remaining vestiges of Indian resistance and Indian autonomy was stronger than ever. By 1890 this would be accomplished.

Garfield and Arthur: Rutherford B. Hayes decided against seeking reelection in 1880. The Republican Party nominated Ohioan James A. Garfield to be their candidate for President. For Vice President, they chose New Yorker Chester A. Arthur. The Republicans were victorious, and on March 4, 1881, Garfield and Arthur assumed their respective offices.

The Garfield Administration was short lived. On July 2, 1881, Garfield was shot by Charles Guiteau. A Republican, Guiteau was angered by his inability to secure a government job in return for his long-time affiliation with the Republican Party. He blamed Garfield. The President held onto life for 80 days, but finally, on September 19, 1881, he died.

The Spoils System: The Garfield assassination turned popular opinion against the so-called spoils system. Under the spoils system, Republicans received government jobs during Republican administrations and Democrats received government jobs during Democrat administrations. Having gained prominence in the late

1820s during the Jackson Administration, the spoils system pervaded not only at the federal level in 1880, but at the state and local levels as well. When the spoils system did not work for Charles Guiteau, Mr. Guiteau decided to vote his man, Garfield, out of office with his pistol. Guiteau's act convinced many Americans that the spoils system had grown way out of hand.

In January 1883, Congress passed the Pendleton Act which stated that merit, not political favoritism, must be the basis for government hiring decisions. President Chester A. Arthur, despite being a past champion of the spoils system, signed the Pendleton Act into law.

Cleveland, Harrison, and Cleveland: Democrats took advantage of increasing factionalism within the stronger Republican Party and put their own man into the White House in 1884. Grover Cleveland is best remembered for his stand on the high import tariffs, which had been in place since the Civil War. Cleveland fought to lower these tariffs, arguing they were detrimental to competition. Cleveland's crusade to lower the tariffs met considerable opposition from both private sector management and labor, who enjoyed the competitive advantage and resulting higher profits and wages the high tariffs provided. This opposition would cost him the 1888 Presidential election.

In the 1888 Presidential election, American industry and the Republican Party cooperated to replace Cleveland with Benjamin Harrison, the grandson of the ninth President of the United States, William Henry Harrison. Harrison served without distinction. In 1892 Harrison was replaced by the man he replaced in 1888, Grover Cleveland. Cleveland served his second term from 1893 to 1897. Cleveland remains the only President in U.S. history to serve nonconsecutive terms in office.

Plessy v. Ferguson: The last nail in the coffin of Congressional Reconstruction was the Supreme Court's *Plessy v. Ferguson* decision. In 1896 the Supreme Court ruled to uphold a Louisiana state law that prohibited blacks from riding in railroad cars designated as "white only." The ruling, known as *Plessy v. Ferguson*, declared that racial segregation enforced at the state and local levels was not a violation of black rights as outlined by the Fourteenth Amendment. The court ruled that black citizens were entitled to "separate but equal" facilities.

The word "equal" was stretched to the limit of its meaning in the aftermath of *Plessy v. Ferguson*. The ruling legitimized the Jim Crow laws, which were on the books throughout the southern states in the 1890s. The Jim Crow laws mandated separation between the races. Blacks could not attend white schools, use white restrooms, eat at white lunch counters and so on. Blacks who failed to heed the Jim Crow laws were subject to criminal prosecution. Although black schools were supposed to be equal in quality and have equivalent resources as white schools, black restrooms were supposed to be maintained with the same care as white restrooms etc... this was clearly not the case in the South in the 1890s and beyond. *Plessy v. Ferguson* would prove that the concept of "separate but equal" does not work.

William McKinley: The Presidential election of 1896 returned the White House to Republican hands. On March 4, 1897, William McKinley was inaugurated the twenty-fifth President of the United States. Immediately after taking office, McKinley faced a foreign policy crisis to the south.

By the turn of the century, the U.S. had grown into a true superpower. In 1823 President James Monroe had established the Monroe Doctrine, which stated the U.S. would not stand for

European muscle-flexing in the Western Hemisphere. For most of the nineteenth century, the U.S. did not have the economic or military strength to enforce the Monroe Doctrine vigorously. By 1897 the United States had developed the strength to enforce the Monroe Doctrine with a vengeance.

The Cuban Rebellion: In the 1890s the Caribbean island of Cuba remained the last vestige of Spain's once great empire in the Americas. In 1895 Cuban revolutionaries struck against their Spanish rulers. Determined to keep hold of Cuba, Spain moved to crush the insurrection. Spain quelled the rebellion successfully but was unable to do so without capturing the attention of the United States.

The Sinking of the *Maine*: In February 1898, McKinley dispatched the *U.S.S. Maine* to Havana Harbor with the expressed purpose of protecting U.S. citizens in Havana, as widespread riots had broken out in the city. On the night of February 15, an explosion of unknown origin rocked the *Maine*, sending her and 250 U.S. sailors to the bottom of Havana Harbor. Although it was not clear that Spain was responsible for the sinking of the *Maine*, the furor created over the incident drove the two nations to war in April 1898.

The Spanish-American War: The first shots of the Spanish-American War were fired not in Cuba, but halfway around the world in another Spanish colony, the Philippines, where six U.S. Navy ships under the command of Commodore Thomas Dewey engaged the seven ship Spanish squadron stationed in Manila. Outgunned and outdated, the Spanish lost all their ships in a seven-hour naval battle just off the coast of Manila on May 1, 1898. U.S. losses were minimal.

Dewey's triumph in the Philippines gave the Americans a tremendous shot in the arm as they launched the invasion of Cuba in June 1898. Setting their sights on Santiago, the Spanish naval base on the southern coast of Cuba, the Americans landed 17,000 troops just west of the city on June 22. Marching east to take the city, the Americans engaged the Spanish in the Battles of El Caney and San Juan Hill on the outskirts of Santiago on July 1. The Americans triumphed in both engagements, forcing the Spanish fleet to evacuate Santiago Bay.

On July 3, 1898, the Spanish fleet was destroyed as it attempted to flee Santiago Bay. Like their comrades at Manila, the Spanish fell victim to superior U.S. Navy firepower. When the four-hour naval battle was over, the Spanish fleet was destroyed, 474 Spanish sailors were either killed or wounded, and 1,750 Spanish sailors were taken prisoner. The U.S. Navy suffered two casualties.

On July 17, 1898, the Spanish ground forces in Santiago, Cuba surrendered to the U.S. Army. On July 26, 1898, Spain requested peace terms, effectively ending the Spanish-American War. The war ended with only 379 U.S. battle deaths. The U.S. gained the former Spanish colonies of Cuba, Puerto Rico, and the Philippines.

The Philippine Insurrection: In the aftermath of the Spanish-American War, Filipinos, who had been grateful to the U.S. for helping them overthrow Spanish rule, were soon at odds with their American liberators. Believing the Americans would help them gain their independence and then leave, the Filipino revolutionaries, who had fought on the side of the U.S. during the Spanish-American War, found themselves fighting against the Americans who had no intention of leaving once the war was over. The Philippine insurrection lasted three years resulting in over 4,000 American deaths and over 20,000 Filipino deaths. Eventually, the U.S. triumphed. The U.S. would remain in control of the Philippines until the Japanese invasion of the islands in World War II.

1900-1932: REFORM, NORMALCY, AND DEPRESSION

By 1900 the U.S. was well on its way to becoming the world's premier economic superpower. Despite the strong economy, a large portion of the nation's population continued to live in squalor. In 1900 half of the nation's adult population was still denied the right to vote. More and more Americans began to realize that the time was right for reform.

A substantial amount of reform legislation was enacted in the early twentieth century. Laws designed to protect the environment, protect the consumer from tainted foods and drugs, and to improve conditions for the nation's workers were implemented between 1900 and 1920. Also, during this period, two prominent amendments, the Eighteenth and Nineteenth Amendments, were added to the U.S. Constitution.

Ratified in 1919, the Eighteenth Amendment prohibited the production, transportation, and sale of intoxicating beverages within the United States. It failed. As alcohol had been part of American history for over 200 years, outlawing it did not make it disappear. Instead of purchasing a pint of beer at the corner tavern, Americans turned to speakeasies, illegal bars run and supplied by such American luminaries as Alphonse Capone and Arnold Rothstein. In 1933 the Eighteenth Amendment would be repealed.

In 1920 the Nineteenth Amendment was ratified, extending the right to vote to the nation's adult women. For nearly 150 years after the birth of the nation, women had been excluded from the political process. After 1920 this was no longer the case.

The reform movement waned a bit during the 1920s, as the nation returned to a "business as usual" attitude. The 1920s would prove to be an era of tremendous prosperity for many. In 1929 it would all come tumbling down with the stock market crash and the onslaught of the Great Depression.

Theodore Roosevelt: New Yorker Theodore Roosevelt became William McKinley's running mate when McKinley successfully sought reelection in 1900. On September 6, 1901, McKinley was shot in Buffalo, New York. Eight days later he died. Subsequently, Theodore Roosevelt became the twenty-sixth President of the United States.

Roosevelt was the first strong U.S. President since Lincoln. As a group, the chief executives in the latter part of the nineteenth century were secondary in importance to Congress, which in turn served the needs of the nation's special interest groups, most notably big business. Early on Roosevelt made it clear that he was the man in charge. He was a believer in a strong central government and is considered by many to be the father of the so-called "Progressive" movement.

The Coal Miners' Strike: In the summer of 1902, 140,000 members of the United Mine Workers went on strike. Underpaid and overworked, the striking coal miners hoped to bring the mine owners to the bargaining table. Refusing to negotiate, the mine owners were content to sit out the strike, confident the federal government would eventually intervene to break the strike rather than face the prospect of a winter without coal. Trying to find a mutually agreeable solution to the crisis, Roosevelt invited both parties to Washington in October 1902. United Mine Workers leader John Mitchell came to the White House ready to make a deal, but the mine owners refused to listen to Mitchell and instead demanded from Roosevelt that he send in federal troops to break the strike. Angered by the owner's recalcitrance, Roosevelt vowed that he would send in troops, not to crush the strike, but to take over the mines from the owners and resume operations under government control. The mine owners took the hint, and a peaceful solution to the strike was soon negotiated.

The resolution of the miners' strike was one in a series of steps Roosevelt took to assert government influence over the economy. Roosevelt was not a socialist, as he did not believe in bringing business under government control. Yet he did feel that, in those instances where the interests of business and the American public conflicted, the government should intervene on the public's behalf.

Trust Busting: With this in mind, Roosevelt moved to break up many of the nation's business trusts. The trusts were groups of corporations, operating in related industries, which colluded together to drive out competitors. The trusts would use their superior size and financial resources to undercut their competitors on price, thereby driving their competitors out of business. Once these competitors were gone, the trusts would raise their prices, thereby enabling themselves to earn exorbitant (monopoly) profits. The owners of the corporations operating within the trusts would amass huge fortunes at the expense of the nation's small businessmen and consumers. Among the trusts dissolved during the Roosevelt Administration were the National Securities Company (a railroad trust), the American Tobacco Company, and John D. Rockefeller's Standard Oil Company.

Other business reforms implemented during the Roosevelt Administration include the Hepburn Act which provided for government regulation of railroad rates, and the Pure Food and

Drug Act which established minimum standards for food and drugs sold in the United States.

The Panama Canal: Roosevelt's aggressiveness was not limited to domestic affairs. One of Roosevelt's greatest achievements was the building of the Panama Canal which greatly reduced the travel time of ships sailing from the East Coast to the West Coast of the United States. When Roosevelt reached a disagreement with Colombia, which controlled the land on which the proposed canal was to be built, he encouraged the people of the Panamanian Region of Colombia to revolt. When Colombian troops rushed to put down the Panamanian Rebellion in November 1903, they were greeted by U.S. troops who persuaded the Colombians to respect the sovereignty of the newly independent state. Thus, the nation of Panama was born, and a favorable treaty was signed with the new Panamanian government which gave the U.S. control over the canal zone.

William Taft: In 1908 the immensely popular Roosevelt chose not to seek reelection. His handpicked successor, Republican William Taft, was easily elected the twenty-seventh President of the United States. Like Roosevelt, Taft was a Progressive. Taft continued the battle against the nation's powerful business trusts. He proved to be an able trust-buster and enjoyed a relatively successful Presidency. Yet his prospects for reelection in 1912 were doomed when his old friend, Theodore Roosevelt, decided he once again wanted to be President.

The Election of 1912: Certain members of the Republican Party could not accept Taft as a viable replacement for their beloved Theodore Roosevelt. This group flocked to Roosevelt when he contested Taft for the Republican Presidential nomination in 1912. Yet Taft did win the nomination at the June Republican National Convention. Angered, Roosevelt and his supporters stormed out of the convention and launched an independent bid for the Presidency on the Bull Moose ticket. In the November Presidential election, Taft and Roosevelt split the Republican vote, enabling Democrat Woodrow Wilson to capture the Presidency.

Woodrow Wilson: Woodrow Wilson continued and expanded upon many of the reforms started by Theodore Roosevelt. In 1914 Wilson set up the Federal Trade Commission to enforce government regulations on firms engaged in interstate trade. In 1914 Wilson gained passage of the Clayton Anti-Trust Act, which forbade common business practices such as discriminatory pricing and having individuals serve on the Board of Directors of competing corporations. The Clayton Act also bolstered the power of the nation's labor unions.

Other legislative reforms implemented by Wilson include the Federal Reserve Act which provided for the first centralized bank in the U.S. since the early 1830s when Andrew Jackson disbanded Hamilton's Bank of the United States and the Underwood Tariff which lowered tariffs on imports, thereby increasing competition and lowering prices for American consumers. Not surprisingly, Wilson was not a favorite among the nation's big business leaders. Yet he did gain support from many of the nation's workers, consumers, and small businessmen, all of whom his reforms were designed to help. This support enabled him to be reelected in 1916.

World War I: Wilson soon found himself distracted from his domestic agenda by a new war which was being waged in Europe. This European war pitted the Allies: Britain, France, and Russia; against the Central Powers: Austria-Hungary, Turkey, and Germany. Determined to stay out of the conflict, Wilson proclaimed U.S. neutrality in August 1914.

Submarine Warfare: The United States would not be able to stay out of World War I. During the war, Germany found that the most valuable weapon in its arsenal was the submarine. From 1914 to 1918 the German Navy conducted all-out submarine warfare against Allied shipping in the North Atlantic. American lives were inevitably lost. In May 1915, 128 Americans died when a German submarine torpedoed the British passenger liner *Lusitania*, just off the coast of Ireland. The *Lusitania* sinking turned American popular opinion against Germany in the war. In January 1917, Germany announced that American ships sailing in the North Atlantic would be subject to attack. Prior to 1917, the Germans had taken great pains to avoid sinking American ships in the North Atlantic for fear of bringing the U.S. into the war against their nation. In response to the German announcement, the U.S. Congress, prompted by President Wilson, declared war on Germany in April 1917.

The European Land Campaign: In June 1917, American ground troops began arriving in France where the European land war was taking place. By the summer of 1918, their participation in the land war was proving decisive. German ground troops, many of whom had spent the last four years of their lives engaged in a war of attrition against the Allies in disease-ridden trenches in northern France, were not prepared to face a large number of fresh American infantry soldiers. On September 26, 1918, the American troops launched the Meuse-Argonne offensive. This offensive was part of an overall Allied attack on the Germans in northern France. The offensive was a costly one for both sides, but when it was over the Allies stood victorious and the German Army was broken. On November 11, 1918, Germany surrendered. On June 28, 1919, the Treaty of Versailles was signed, officially ending World War I.

The Aftermath of World War I: The effects of World War I on the men and nations involved were profound. The war effort proved too costly for the Russian leader, Czar Nicholas II. Weakened by the war, the Czar was forced to abdicate his throne in March 1917. After a brief power struggle, the Bolsheviks (Communists) assumed control of the nation in November 1917 and immediately made peace with the Germans. Thus, the Soviet Union was born.

The terms dictated to Germany by the victorious Allies in the Treaty of Versailles were onerous and helped to create a politically unstable environment in that nation after the war. Designed to keep Germany weak, the Treaty of Versailles undermined the ability of the post-war German government to keep order within Germany itself. As a result, chaos would rule in Germany following World War I. One man, Adolf Hitler, would rise from this chaos, promising to return order and pride to the German nation. Hitler and his Nazi cohorts would come to rule Germany in the early 1930s. By 1940 Hitler would bring the horror of war back to the European continent.

Women's Suffrage: As of 1920, the nation's women were without the right to vote nationwide. In the 1840s and 1850s prominent Abolitionists Elizabeth Cady Stanton, Lucretia Mott, and Susan B. Anthony began pushing for women's rights, most prominent of which was the guaranteed right to vote or "suffrage." Their cause gained some traction but soon became overshadowed by the U.S. Civil War. Regaining momentum would take time. The women's suffrage movement's first gains came in the West. Women gained the right to vote in the Wyoming Territory in 1869 and Colorado became the first state to guarantee women's suffrage in 1893. Finally, in 1920 the Nineteenth Amendment was ratified, mandating women's voting rights nationwide.

Harding and Coolidge: In 1920 the Republicans nominated Ohioan Warren G. Harding to be their candidate for President. Tired of reform, Americans found appeal in Harding's promise to "return to normalcy." Consequently, on election day the conservative Harding trounced his Democrat opponent to become the twenty-ninth President of the United States.

Harding was a "hands-off" President, both with regards to the national economy and running his own administration. Believing that government had become too involved in the affairs of business, Harding adopted a laissez-faire or "let them be" attitude toward the nation's large corporations. Trust-busting and strict enforcement of regulations were swept aside during the Harding Administration.

Unfortunately for Harding, he also adopted a laissez-faire attitude towards the top officials within his own administration. A basically honest man himself, Harding was, nonetheless, surrounded by crooks. His Attorney General, Harry Daugherty, was accused of selling pardons to convicted criminals and receiving bribes from moonshiners. His Secretary of the Interior, Albert Fall, was convicted of accepting a bribe in return for turning over drilling rights to the Teapot Dome oil reserve, situated in Wyoming, to a private oil company. The oil reserve at Teapot Dome was supposed to serve as an emergency fuel supply for the U.S. military.

On August 2, 1923, Harding died before the full extent of his administration's corruption became known to the American public. Fortunately, the new President, Calvin Coolidge, had been one of the honest members of the Harding administration while he had served as Vice President. Coolidge continued Harding's laissez-faire approach to the economy, and during his administration the economy boomed.

Herbert Hoover: Calvin Coolidge decided against seeking the Republican nomination in 1928. The Republicans nominated

Californian Herbert Hoover who trounced his Democrat opponent in the 1928 Presidential election. The thirty-first President of the United States entered office at a time of tremendous prosperity. The nation's factories were turning out goods in record numbers. The wealthy were growing wealthier and more numerous. The speculative craze of the late 1920s had pushed the nation's stock market to dizzying heights. On October 24, 1929, it all came tumbling down.

The Stock Market Crash: On Black Thursday, October 24, 1929, the U.S. stock market crashed. Within three weeks stock investors had lost over $30 billion. As it was common for investors to borrow heavily to purchase stocks, many were completely wiped out as the value of their stocks plummeted during the Crash of 1929. Additionally, the nation's banks, which had lent money to investors to purchase these stocks, found themselves unable to recoup their loans as their paper collateral deflated in value. Banks began to fail. As deposits were uninsured by the government in 1929, depositors throughout the nation responded to the crisis by running to their own banks to withdraw their money, for fear of losing their savings. This process snowballed, resulting in bank failures throughout the nation. By 1930 the nation was heading straight for economic depression, a depression which would last for a decade.

The Great Depression: A good analogy for the Great Depression is that of a snowball rolling down a snow-covered hill, constantly getting bigger and gaining momentum. Speculators, who had lost everything in the Crash of 1929, drastically cut back their consumption of goods and services. With consumer demand lagging, the providers of goods and services, in turn, laid off their employees which resulted in a further decrease in consumer demand. Even those who remained employed would cut back their purchases because they too feared that they would soon lose their jobs. Despite the ever-worsening economic crisis, President Hoover was determined to let the economy run its natural course with minimal government interference. Hoover tried to arouse confidence in the American people, telling them repeatedly that, "prosperity is just around the corner." Yet by 1932 over 12 million Americans were unemployed, the nation's output was two-thirds of what it was in 1928, and consumer confidence was nonexistent.

The RFC: In January 1932 Hoover finally acted, establishing the Reconstruction Finance Corporation to help battle the Depression. The RFC provided government loans to banks, state and local governments, and railroad companies. The hope was that these government loans would encourage the building of roads, bridges, and railroads, thereby putting the unemployed to work. The RFC pumped about $2 billion into the economy, which was not a small chunk of change in 1932. Nevertheless, the RFC proved to be too little too late for Hoover. By 1932 the Depression was too severe to be much affected by the RFC. In the 1932 Presidential election, Hoover was trounced by Democrat Franklin Delano Roosevelt, who promised desperate Americans a "New Deal."

1933-1945: THE ROOSEVELT YEARS

Franklin Delano Roosevelt (FDR) assumed the Presidency on March 4, 1933. He entered office at a low point in American history. Americans were hurting economically, their confidence in the nation had been badly shaken, and they faced the future with trepidation. In his inaugural address FDR proclaimed to the nation, **"The only thing we have to fear is fear itself**." The next day he went to work implementing his plan to provide the nation with economic relief, recovery, and reform, his so-called New Deal.

Banking Reform: Roosevelt knew that before any recovery could take place public confidence in the nation's banking system would have to be restored. The day after his inauguration FDR declared a four day "bank holiday" during which time all the nation's banks were closed. During the holiday Congress passed, and FDR signed into law, the Emergency Banking Act which ultimately put the nation's banks under federal control. After the bank holiday Roosevelt allowed those banks deemed to be solvent to reopen.

In June 1933 FDR signed the Glass-Steagall Act into law which greatly increased government regulation of the nation's banking system. Glass-Steagall curtailed the ability of banks to engage in speculative activities which, in large part, had contributed to the banking crisis in the aftermath of the Stock Market Crash of 1929. Also, Glass-Steagall established the Federal Deposit Insurance Corporation which provided government insurance for individual bank deposits. By creating the FDIC, Roosevelt hoped to send the message to the citizens that banks were indeed a safe place to keep their savings. He succeeded.

New Deal Jobs Programs: Roosevelt looked to attack unemployment by placing many of the nation's unemployed directly on the federal payroll. In March 1933 FDR established the Civilian Conservation Corps. The CCC provided the nation's young unemployed men with room, board, and a nominal wage. In return the men were put to work planting trees, improving the national parks, and building roads. The CCC would remain in operation up until World War II. In November 1933 Roosevelt established the Civil Works Administration. The CWA employed 4 million individuals over the 1933-1934 winter, repairing roads, shoveling snow, etc... Critics claimed that the CWA projects were mostly unnecessary and in March 1934 the CWA was disbanded.

New Deal Social Welfare Programs: To help alleviate the suffering of those who remained unemployed, FDR established the Federal Emergency Relief Administration in May 1933. FERA gave direct grants to state and local governments which, in turn, made the funds available to their citizens in need. FERA provided the basis for many of the nation's current social welfare programs.

Social Security: To aid the nation's elderly, many of whom had lost some or all their life's savings in the Stock Market Crash and the subsequent bank failures, Roosevelt gained passage of the Social Security Act in August 1935. The Social Security Act provided monthly payments to the nation's retired citizens over 65. To finance Social Security Roosevelt implemented a nationwide payroll tax. Although it was created as a simple Depression-era senior relief program, Social Security **has evolved to become the centerpiece of the U.S. retirement system**. Social Security was designed as a "pay-as-you-go" program. This means that current workers pay Social Security taxes into the government and that money goes immediately back out to current beneficiaries. There is no real built-in savings mechanism. **This DESIGN FLAW would**

have severe consequences to America's financial health at all levels down the road.

The NRA: To help boost employment in the private business sector, FDR established the National Recovery Administration in June 1933. The NRA was designed to be a vehicle for government and business to work together to bring an end to the Depression. The NRA established codes of conduct for firms which chose to join. Roosevelt hoped that NRA codes, such as those limiting workweeks to 40 hours and abolishing child labor, would force firms to hire additional adult workers. Although NRA membership was optional, FDR used his influence as President to encourage American consumers to patronize firms which were NRA members. The implication was that American firms which chose not to join the NRA should not be patronized. For many firms this meant mandatory membership in the NRA. The NRA remained in operation until May 1935 when the Supreme Court ruled it unconstitutional.

The PWA: Also in June 1933 FDR established the Public Works Administration. The PWA worked with state and local governments to provide funds to private firms for the building of roads, bridges, tunnels, and government buildings. Benefits from the PWA were twofold. Able-bodied adults were put to work and the nation's infrastructure was greatly improved.

Relief for Farmers: For farmers, who had been adversely affected by low agricultural prices, FDR established the Agricultural Adjustment Administration in May 1933. The AAA provided government subsidies to farmers for holding back a portion of their land from production. The AAA was successful in curtailing agricultural supply, thereby driving up agricultural prices. This made the AAA unpopular among city dwellers, as it brought about higher food prices. It also struck many Americans as odd that their government was paying farmers not to grow food when so many in the nation were going to bed hungry every night. The AAA remained in effect until January 1936, when the Supreme Court ruled it unconstitutional.

The WPA: Although New Deal programs were having some effect on unemployment and the economy, the Depression continued into 1935. In May 1935 FDR established the Works Progress Administration. The WPA employed millions through the early 1940s building airfields, roads, schools, and other government structures. Like the PWA, the WPA not only increased employment but helped to improve the nation's infrastructure. However, the WPA did not limit its efforts to construction. The WPA also financed the work of the nation's artists, musicians, and actors. This government financing of the arts helped to give the WPA its image as a wasteful "make work" institution in the minds of many conservative Americans.

Other New Deal Programs: Roosevelt implemented several other New Deal programs. The Farm Credit Act of 1933 provided government refinancing for farmers who were in danger of having their farms repossessed by their banks. The Home Owners Loan Corporation, established in 1933, provided the same service for homeowners in trouble. In 1934 the Federal Housing Administration was established to provide government insurance for home loans made by banks to individuals who otherwise would not have the credit to secure private financing. The Tennessee Valley Authority, established in 1933, constructed and ran many dams and powerplants in Tennessee, North Carolina, and Alabama. The TVA brought electricity to the region as well as jobs.

The Legacy of the New Deal: Looking back at Roosevelt's New Deal programs, one cannot deny that they had immediate and lasting effects on American society. Although Roosevelt was not completely successful in removing the nation's economic woes as the economy continued to struggle into the 1940s, he did put Americans to work who otherwise would have remained unemployed and he did provide relief for those worst hit by the poor economic conditions. Certain reforms initiated during his Administration would have a lasting effect on the American economy. For example, the 1933 Glass-Steagall Banking Act limited greatly the amount of risk the nation's banks could assume, thereby helping to create stability within the nation's banking industry (all the way up to 2008). This stability would prove to be essential as the nation's economy began to grow anew in the late 1930s and would continue to grow in the 1940s and 1950s. Also several of Roosevelt's programs helped to create tangible items which have remained useful to Americans to the present day. Numerous schools, post offices, bridges, and countless miles of roads were constructed through New Deal programs.

Perhaps the most important legacy of Roosevelt's New Deal is that of **big government and big government spending**. Prior to his taking office, the federal government's debt was less than $20 billion. By 1940 the federal debt had ballooned to $43 billion. By today's standards this increase seems minor, but, nonetheless, it set a crucial precedent. Roosevelt introduced the nation to big government and deficit spending, and both would remain in place in the U.S. long after the New Deal and Roosevelt's Presidency.

FDR's View of Public Sector Unions: Despite being a Progressive Icon Roosevelt was very wary of public sector unions and collective bargaining between elected officials and government employees. FDR realized that government employees have a major say as voters and donors as to who would be on the other side of the negotiating table. Private sector managers have a strong incentive to negotiate tough but fair deals with Labor. Elected officials do not. **Rather, politicians have a strong incentive to placate a very motivated special interest group (i.e., public sector labor unions).** FDR foresaw the plethora of bad deals politicians would strike with public sector union leaders for the remainder of the 20th Century and beyond.

Build-up to World War II: The event which would bring a decisive end to the Depression in the U.S. was World War II. In the 1930s three nations would establish themselves as powerful threats to peace and liberty. The so-called Axis Powers (Japan, Germany, and, to a much lesser extent, Italy) would spread a reign of terror throughout the globe that would result in a massive loss of life and immeasurable human suffering. The Axis Powers would provide the ultimate test for the world's premier superpower.

Japan: In 1931 Japan invaded the Manchuria region of northeast China. The Japanese moved against the rest of China in 1937. The U.S. expressed concern over the Japanese aggression in China but fell short of threatening force. In July 1941 Japan continued its quest for domination over the Far East by invading French Indochina. This invasion caused Roosevelt to freeze Japanese assets in the United States and suspend U.S.-Japanese trade. Yet the U.S., desiring to avert war with Japan, would continue to try to keep the peace with the renegade Asian nation through December 6, 1941.

Italy: In 1935 Italian dictator Benito Mussolini launched the invasion of Ethiopia in Africa. In 1939 he took Albania in southeastern Europe. Although he was an aggressive despot, Mussolini would prove not to be as formidable a threat to peace and freedom as his neighbor to the north. In 1943 the Italian public would tire of Mr. Mussolini's totalitarian and warring ways and kick him out of office.

Germany: The mayhem in post-World War I Germany gave rise to one man, Adolf Hitler, who would prove to be the most powerful threat to freedom and liberty in the twentieth century. Taking control of Germany in 1933, Hitler and his Nazi cronies quickly went to work rearming Germany in defiance of the 1919 Treaty of Versailles. Once he had rearmed his nation, Hitler began his campaign to conquer Europe. In 1936 German troops marched across the Rhine River to occupy the Rhineland, the buffer area between Germany and France which had been demilitarized since World War I. In March 1938 Hitler and his troops swallowed up Austria.

Appeasement at Munich: When Hitler moved to take the Sudetenland region of Czechoslovakia in September 1938 the other European superpowers, Britain and France, finally demanded that Hitler curtail his quest for Europe. On September 30, 1938 Hitler, British Prime Minister Neville Chamberlain, and French Prime Minister Edouard Daladier met in Munich, Germany. The Munich meeting was a last attempt by Britain and France to avert war with their land grabbing neighbor. As a result of the meeting the Munich Pact was signed in which France and Britain agreed to let Hitler take the Sudetenland region of Czechoslovakia in return for Hitler's promise that he would make no further territorial claims in Europe. British Prime Minister Chamberlain stated that, by appeasing Hitler's demand for German occupation of the Sudetenland, the Munich Pact would assure, "peace in our time."

Chamberlain was wrong. Not satisfied with just the Sudetenland, Hitler took all of Czechoslovakia in March 1939, in violation of the Munich Pact. France and Britain did nothing. In August 1939 Hitler and Soviet leader Joseph Stalin signed a non-aggression pact. Under terms of the pact the two men agreed to split the nation of Poland between them. On September 1, 1939 Hitler launched the German invasion of Poland, which fell within the month. On September 3, 1939 Britain and France, having guaranteed to protect Poland from Hitler, reluctantly declared war on Germany. World War II was underway.

The European Campaign (1940-1941): After the invasion of Poland, Europe was quiet during the winter of 1939-1940, except for Hitler's ally, Stalin, who took advantage of the lull to invade the Baltic states (Lithuania, Latvia, and Estonia) and attempt to invade Finland. The so-called "sitting war" was shattered when Hitler invaded Denmark and Norway in April 1940. With Denmark and Norway in hand Hitler invaded Luxembourg, the Netherlands, and Belgium in May. Soon the German "blitzkrieg" (lightning war) reached the French countryside. The British and French troops defending France were thoroughly defeated by the fast-moving Germans. Between May 26 and June 4 roughly 340,000 British, French and Belgian troops were evacuated from the beaches of Dunkirk, in northwest France, to Britain. On June 22, 1940 France surrendered to Hitler.

The Battle of Britain: Next Hitler set his sights on Britain. In July 1940 Hitler began the Battle of Britain, a four-month air war, during which much of London was reduced to rubble. However, Hitler had a new foe in Britain, Winston Churchill, who had replaced Chamberlain as Prime Minister that March. The British persevered. The Royal Air Force destroyed over 1,800 German Air Force planes during the Battle of Britain, forcing Hitler to postpone permanently his plans to invade the island nation.

The Invasion of the Soviet Union: In June 1941 Hitler launched the German invasion of the Soviet Union despite the non-aggression pact he had signed with Soviet dictator Stalin two years earlier. By conquering the eastern half of the Soviet Union, Hitler hoped to increase the "lebensraum" (living room) of the German nation. Although the invasion began well for Hitler as his troops reached the outskirts of Moscow by December, his inability to conquer the Soviet Union before winter would cost him the war. As the temperature dropped and the snows fell, the Soviet Army began a vicious counterattack on the German forces. Winter fighting was the forte of the Soviet Army. The poorly clothed and sheltered German troops had to fight not only the Soviet Army but hypothermia as well. Ordered by Hitler to hold their ground, the German Army suffered a staggering number of casualties during the winter of 1941-1942. Although the bulk of the German Army survived the winter of 1941-1942 and made impressive gains the following summer, they again failed to break Joseph Stalin and the Soviet Army before the onslaught of winter. The bitter winter of 1942-1943 would turn the tide against Hitler on the eastern front.

U.S. Views Toward the War: Following World War I the U.S. entered a stage of extreme isolationism. European and Asian problems were thought best to be left to the Europeans and Asians. Even as Hitler trampled Europe and the Japanese conquered the Far East, Americans remained determined to stay out of the war. Perhaps the spirit of isolationism was best exemplified by the popularly supported Ludlow Amendment which called for a national referendum before the U.S. government would be allowed to declare war. If the Ludlow Amendment had passed, the Congress and the President would have been required to secure direct permission from the American electorate before committing U.S. military forces to war. The amendment was narrowly defeated by the House in January 1938, but its message was heard loud and clear by Roosevelt. The American public did not want to get involved in yet another foreign war.

Roosevelt's View Toward the War: Roosevelt realized early on that the Axis Powers would have to be stopped and that the U.S. would have to play an active role in ensuring this was done. In October 1937 Roosevelt equated Japanese and German imperialism to a disease that needed to be quarantined. Yet Roosevelt had to be sensitive to American public opinion which was extremely against becoming militarily involved in either Europe or Asia. Roosevelt had his work cut out for him to sway public opinion in the other direction.

Lend-Lease: Germany's capture of France and the vicious bombing of London in 1940 alerted many Americans to the dangers of Hitler and Nazism. In the summer of 1940 Congress appropriated funds for the establishment of a two-ocean navy. In the years 1940-1945 the U.S. would produce over 1,200 naval ships and nearly 300,000 military aircraft, an astounding feat for the burgeoning Superpower. In March 1941 Roosevelt signed the Lend-Lease Act into law. Lend-Lease enabled Roosevelt to supply Britain and later the Soviet Union with sorely needed war materials. Despite the passage of these bills, Congress and the public remained firmly against direct American intervention. Public opinion would change dramatically on December 7, 1941.

The Attack on Pearl Harbor: On the morning of December 7, 1941 the Japanese staged a surprise air attack against U.S. military forces at Pearl Harbor, Hawaii. Over 2,400 Americans were killed in the attack. Nineteen U.S. warships were sunk or disabled. Over 180 U.S. planes were destroyed, most on the ground. Tactically the attack on Pearl Harbor was a great success for the Japanese. From a historical perspective, Pearl Harbor marked the beginning of the end for the Axis Powers.

American Sentiment Shifts: Nobody knows for certain if the United States would have eventually fought in World War II had it not been for the Pearl Harbor attack. Through December 6, 1941 most Americans remained strongly isolationist. On December 7, 1941 this spirit of isolationism evaporated. When Roosevelt appeared before a joint session of Congress on December 8, 1941, to ask for a declaration of war against Japan, Congress overwhelmingly voted for the declaration. Within the week the U.S. was at war with Germany and Italy as well. The Allied Forces led by Britain, the Soviet Union, and now the United States were fully formed.

The Japanese American Internments: Following the attack on Pearl Harbor, Roosevelt authorized the forced relocation of 120,000 Japanese Americans, living on the West Coast of the United States. Although the majority of those rounded up had been born in the United States, these Japanese Americans, according to the Washington policymakers, posed a security threat. For over three years the Japanese Americans would be confined to detention camps in the interior of the United States.

The North African Campaign: The first American land action against the Germans came in November 1942 in North Africa. U.S. troops landed in Morocco and Algeria to aid British troops, led by General Bernard Montgomery, in their fight against German General Erwin Rommel's North Africa Corps. U.S. General George S. Patton took command of the U.S. forces and his presence proved decisive. By May 1943 North Africa was firmly in Allied hands.

The European Campaign: The U.S. with the help of its allies looked next to re-establish a foothold on the Continent of Europe. 1943 was a tremendous year for British and U.S. air power, which wreaked havoc on German industry and the German Air Force. Crippled, the Germans, nonetheless, put up a strong fight when the

Allies began their invasion of Sicily in July 1943 and the Italian mainland in September 1943. The quest for Italy went much slower than the Allies had hoped. It was not until June 1944 that Rome fell to the Allies; however, combined with the Soviet Army in the East, the Allied troops fighting in Italy kept the bulk of German ground forces occupied while the main Allied attack force was approaching the northwest coast of France.

D-Day: On June 6, 1944 the Allies, led by U.S. General Dwight D. Eisenhower, staged a massive early morning assault on the Normandy beaches of northwest France. The D-Day attack ended with the Allies firmly footed on French soil. By October the superior Allied force had driven the bulk of the German occupying force out of France. It helped that Soviet troops were killing German troops on a massive scale in the East (as they sustained tremendous losses of their own). The German troops retreating on the western front fought hard and made one devastating counterattack against the Allies in December's Battle of the Bulge. Yet by 1945 Hitler was a defeated man. With the Soviets closing in on his east, the Allies battering his armies in the south and west, and most of his nation bombed to rubble, Hitler retreated to the underground of Berlin and shot himself to death. On May 7, 1945 Germany surrendered.

The Holocaust: As Europe was being liberated in late 1944 and early 1945, the atrocious nature of Hitler and Nazism was made clear for all to see. The Allies liberated the camps of Auschwitz, Dachau, and Buchenwald, where the Nazi death machine had been running for the past several years. Prior to the war part of Hitler's appeal to many Germans had been his venomous racist rhetoric. As the war came to a close, Americans learned that Hitler's promise to "cleanse Europe" had not been an empty one. Over six million European Jews were murdered as a result of what has become known as the Holocaust. Millions of others including Slavs, Gypsies, and those who either did or could have posed a threat to Nazism were similarly murdered. Of history's numerous atrocities none have had a greater magnitude or viciousness than Europe's Holocaust.

The Pacific War: While Japanese planes were attacking Pearl Harbor on December 7, 1941, other Japanese forces were preparing to attack American bases on Wake Island, Guam, and the Philippines in the South Pacific. On December 8, 1941 Guam was attacked. On December 23 Wake Island fell. The 75,000 American and Filipino troops defending the Philippines held out until May 1942 when they were finally forced to surrender to the Japanese. Luckily, the commander of U.S. military forces in the Far East, General Douglas MacArthur, escaped from the Philippines before its fall. MacArthur left the Philippines reluctantly, pledging, "I shall return." He would keep his promise.

The Battle of Coral Sea: In May 1942 the American aircraft carriers *Lexington* and *Yorktown* met the Japanese Fleet at the Battle of Coral Sea. In a battle fought exclusively with carrier-based warplanes, the men of the aircraft carriers *Lexington* and *Yorktown* stopped the Japanese from carrying through with their plan to invade Australia. However, the American victory did not come without a price. The *Lexington* was sunk, and the *Yorktown* was badly damaged.

The Battle of Midway: In June 1942 the U.S. Navy, tipped off to expect a Japanese naval attack on Midway Island, met the Japanese Navy once again at the Battle of Midway. The battle was a decisive American victory. American planes sank four Japanese carriers. The battle was a blow from which the Japanese Navy would not recover. Battered at the Battle of the Coral Sea, the U.S. carrier *Yorktown* was nevertheless an instrumental part of the American victory at

Midway. However, the *Yorktown* did not survive the Battle of Midway.

MacArthur Returns: American ground troops led by MacArthur began a counteroffensive in the summer of 1942 which focused on eradicating the Japanese, island by island, from the South Pacific. In August U.S. Marines landed on Guadalcanal, northeast of Australia. After five months of fierce fighting, the last of the Japanese were forced off the island. U.S. troops moved on to other islands and in the autumn of 1944 were in position to retake the Philippines. On October 20, 1944, American troops led by MacArthur landed on Leyte Island in the Philippines. MacArthur's landing was followed by a tremendous American naval victory in the Battle of Leyte Gulf. After five months of bloody fighting, MacArthur's men conquered the last of the Japanese forces in the Philippines.

The Atomic Bomb: In early 1945 U.S. forces captured the islands of Iwo Jima and Okinawa. Both islands were part of Japan itself, and both victories came with an incredible loss of life on both sides. As MacArthur planned for the invasion of the main Japanese islands in the summer of 1945, it became clear to most Americans that subsequent land victories would come only with a severe loss of American lives. In April 1945, President Roosevelt died soon after beginning his fourth term as President. Upon taking office, Harry S. Truman learned of the top-secret Manhattan Project. Begun in 1942, the Manhattan Project employed America's best scientific minds with the task of creating a workable atomic bomb. By the summer of 1945 these scientists had successfully completed their task. On August 6, 1945 the U.S. bomber *Enola Gay* dropped an atomic bomb on the Japanese city of Hiroshima. The city was destroyed. On August 9, 1945 a second atomic bomb destroyed the Japanese city of Nagasaki. The Japanese requested peace terms the following day. On September 2, 1945 Japan officially surrendered to the United States.

The Aftermath of World War II: As the war was ending in Europe, the seeds for a new war were being sewn. By the war's end eastern Europe was controlled by the Soviet Army. Britain, France, and the U.S. controlled the West. Unwilling to cede his territorial gains, Soviet leader Joseph Stalin set up puppet governments in the eastern states, effectively erecting an "iron curtain" between communist eastern Europe and non-communist western Europe. Stalin's promise to conduct legitimate elections in eastern Europe would prove to be an empty one. The western powers were outraged, but not overly surprised, by Stalin's actions following the war. By the late 1940s a new, non-shooting, but nonetheless bitter war was being waged. The Cold War pitted the western free powers led by the U.S., Britain, and France against the eastern totalitarian powers controlled by the Soviet Union. The Cold War would last for the next forty years.

The United Nations: Another product of World War II was the United Nations. Early in the war, the Allied leaders began to discuss the possibility of creating a worldwide organization dedicated to the promotion and preservation of peace throughout the world. The Allied leaders hoped that such an organization would lessen the probability of another major war, a World War III, from breaking out. In June 1945, over 300 countries participated in the drafting of the United Nations charter. In January 1946, the first meeting of the U.N. General Assembly took place in London. In 1949 the U.N. moved into its permanent headquarters in New York City.

1946-1980: THE COLD WAR

The three dominant themes of post-World War II American history are communism, civil rights, and technology. Containing communism would be the foremost U.S. foreign policy goal during this period. The arms race and U.S. participation in the Korean and the Vietnam Wars are products of this foreign policy. Improving civil rights for all Americans would again become a national priority, especially in the 1950s and 1960s. Finally, developments in technology during this short period of time would be nothing less than astounding. Supercomputers, jumbo jets, lunar excursion modules, and VCRs are all products of this period. Satellite technology combined with the television would make possible the instantaneous and widespread dissemination of information.

Harry S. Truman and Containment: Shortly after the dust settled from World War II, the U.S. was engulfed in another war, the Cold War. Stalin's conduct in eastern Europe and the immediate chill in U.S.-Soviet relations following the war made many Americans wary of the "Reds." Responding to the dubious Soviet behavior in eastern Europe following the war, the President issued the **Truman Doctrine** in March 1947. In his address to Congress Truman declared, "I believe that it must be the policy of the United States to support free peoples who are resisting attempted subjugation by armed minorities or by outside pressures." The line was drawn in the sand. The U.S. would spend the next forty plus years working to contain communism.

The Marshall Plan: Europe was left in tatters following World War II. Not wanting to see communism spread to western Europe,

Truman enacted the Marshall Plan in 1947. The Marshall Plan provided direct U.S. economic support to the western European nations as well as Japan. Truman hoped that, by bringing economic stability to western Europe, support for the region's more radical political factions would be undermined. Truman wisely recalled that economic instability in post-World War I Germany had played a decisive role in Hitler's rise to power in that nation. He noted that economic and political chaos tend to run in pairs. Truman did not want to repeat the mistake of his predecessors.

NATO: In 1949 nine European nations along with the United States, Canada, and Iceland signed the North Atlantic Treaty. Thus, the North Atlantic Treaty Organization (NATO) was established. NATO guaranteed each of its members complete and unconditional support should they be attacked by another power. For example, a foreign power set on attacking NATO member Iceland could expect a full retaliatory response from NATO members such as Britain, France, and the United States.

NATO marked a significant change in U.S. foreign policy. Traditionally Americans had been wary of *entangling* foreign alliances. Yet the threat of communism created so much consternation in the U.S. following World War II that Americans seemed willing to scrap isolationism for good. If communism were to be stopped most Americans realized that the U.S. would have to lead the opposition.

The Berlin Airlift: The Cold War grew more bitter in 1948 and 1949. Following the war, the former German capital of Berlin was jointly occupied by the western forces of Britain, France, and the U.S., as well as by the Soviet Union. The western forces occupying West Berlin were surrounded by the Soviets who controlled the east German countryside. In June 1948 Stalin cut off West Berlin's land supply lines from West Germany hoping the blockade would force the evacuation of the French, British, and American troops who were protecting the city. Truman responded to the crisis by enacting the Berlin airlift. For nearly a year the entire city of West Berlin was supplied with food, clothing, and other materials brought over from West Germany by U.S. and British supply planes. In May 1949 Stalin lifted the blockade, realizing that the West was determined not to let West Berlin fall.

The Red Scare: By enacting the Marshall Plan and NATO, and by staring down Stalin at Berlin, Truman made real progress in his struggle to contain communism. Yet there were setbacks. In 1949 the giant Asian nation of China fell to the communists led by Mao Tse Tung. In 1949 the Soviets detonated their first atomic bomb, officially ending the nuclear monopoly of the United States. These events helped to give rise to the "red scare" in the United States. One man would prove to be particularly skillful in exploiting the public's fear of communism.

Joe McCarthy: Wisconsin Senator Joseph McCarthy first made a name for himself in February 1950, when he claimed to have possession of a list of card-carrying communists within the U.S. State Department. Although he never released his list, McCarthy's claim that the communists were everywhere throughout American government and society found appeal on many levels in the United States. From 1950 to 1954 McCarthy led a congressional witch hunt of government agencies and the private sector to ferret out communist sympathizers. Critics of McCarthy and his methods were mostly silent for fear of being labeled as communist sympathizers themselves. Finally, in 1954, when McCarthy accused the U.S. Army of being a bastion for communists, the American public began to realize that his accusations were mostly groundless and irresponsible. In December 1954 McCarthy was censured by his fellow senators for conduct unbecoming a United States senator.

The Korean War: The first true test of the Truman Doctrine came on the Korean Peninsula in Asia. In June 1950, North Korea's communist leader, Kim Il-Sung, launched an invasion of non-communist South Korea. The North caught the South completely by surprise and soon had overrun all of South Korea, less a small area around the southeast Korean city of Pusan. With United Nations backing President Truman sent General Douglas MacArthur to the Korean Peninsula to aid South Korea in its fight.

On September 15, 1950 a United Nations force led by MacArthur landed at the port of Inchon, Korea, well behind the North Korean lines. The U.N. force, composed mainly of U.S. troops, wreaked havoc on the North Korean Army. By November 1950, MacArthur had not only recaptured South Korea but had the North Korean Army pinned against the Yalu River on the North Korean-Chinese border. Then, on November 26, 1950, the Chinese Army entered the conflict, staging a massive counterattack on MacArthur's forces. The Chinese pushed the U.N. force south from the Yalu River. By the summer of 1951 after months of attacks and counterattacks, the line between North and South was fairly well established at the 38th parallel. For the next two years, the war would be fought indecisively along the 38th parallel until an armistice was signed in July 1953.

Truman Fires MacArthur: MacArthur was critical of Truman's desire to keep the Korean War a limited affair. MacArthur wanted to attack China itself once the Chinese had entered the conflict on the side of North Korea. Truman disagreed, fearing that a direct U.S. attack on China would escalate the war to an unacceptable level. MacArthur began to criticize Truman's policy publicly. To Truman,

MacArthur's open opposition to his Commander in Chief was insubordination. On April 11, 1951, Truman relieved MacArthur of his command. Although Truman was justified in his action, he did not enjoy near the popularity MacArthur enjoyed with the American public. As a result of the firing, MacArthur's popularity reached cosmic dimensions, and Truman's limited popularity grew more limited. The MacArthur incident was undoubtedly a large factor in Truman's decision not to seek reelection in 1952.

Dwight D. Eisenhower: World War II hero Dwight D. Eisenhower returned the White House to Republican hands. Eisenhower, who enjoyed immense popularity as a result of his military service, soundly defeated Democrat Adlai Stevenson in the 1952 Presidential election. A devout anti-communist, Eisenhower was also a fiscal conservative. Eisenhower believed that the most cost-effective way to check the spread of communism was to build up the nation's arsenal of nuclear weapons. As the United States enjoyed a virtual nuclear monopoly in the early 1950s, the threat of an all-out American nuclear attack was fairly successful in keeping Soviet misbehavior in check. However, this threat of massive nuclear retaliation grew less effective, and more dangerous, as the Soviets built up their own nuclear arsenal. Eisenhower's desire to have a better way of quickly evacuating the nation's major cities in case of a Soviet nuclear attack was a big factor in his move to start building the interstate highway system in 1956.

The Missile Gap: In October 1957, the Soviets launched the Sputnik satellite into the Earth's orbit. An innocuous little satellite, Sputnik, nonetheless, aroused widespread fear in the United States which had not yet successfully launched a satellite of its own. If the Soviets had the rocket technology to put a satellite into orbit, how long would it take them to develop a rocket which could deliver a nuclear device from the Soviet Union to the mainland United States?

The perception of a "missile gap" pushed Eisenhower into action. In January 1958, the U.S. Army launched America's first satellite, Explorer I. In July 1958, Eisenhower established the National Aeronautics and Space Administration (NASA) which was charged with the task of developing American rocket technology. The missile race was underway. A happier side benefit was that so was the race to the Moon, a race the U.S. would win definitively a mere eleven years later.

Realizing the world was becoming an ever more dangerous place, Eisenhower also worked to improve U.S.-Soviet relations. The death of Soviet strongman Joseph Stalin in 1953 brought more moderate leadership to the Soviet Union. In July 1955 Eisenhower met with the Soviet leaders in Geneva, Switzerland. Although little of a tangible nature was accomplished, the symbolism alone of having the leaders of the free and communist worlds meet was seen as a positive. In September 1959 Eisenhower hosted Soviet leader Nikita Khrushchev to a week-long visit in the United States. Khrushchev's visit was capped by a meeting with Eisenhower at the Presidential retreat at Camp David. During the meeting the two men agreed to meet again the following year at a summit where they would discuss tangible issues. This meeting would not take place.

The U-2 Incident: The summit between Eisenhower and Khrushchev was scheduled to start on May 16, 1960, in Paris. On May 1, 1960 a U.S. U-2 spy plane flown by Francis Gary Powers was shot down over the Soviet Union. Eisenhower admitted that Powers was on a military surveillance mission for the United States but refused Khrushchev's demand for a formal apology. Consequently, Khrushchev announced that the Soviet Union would not participate in the Paris Summit and withdrew an invitation for Eisenhower to visit the Soviet Union later that year. A potential thaw in the Cold War was halted.

Brown v. Board of Education: The 1950s saw a resurgence of the civil rights movement. In its May 1954 decision in the case of *Brown v. Board of Education of Topeka*, the Supreme Court ruled that the nation's public schools must be racially desegregated. The ruling invalidated the 1896 *Plessy v. Ferguson* ruling which had stated that segregating blacks from whites was not a violation of the Fourteenth Amendment to the Constitution. The *Brown v. Board of Education* ruling stirred widespread dissent, especially in the former Confederate states. In September 1957 when nine black students attempted to enroll at Central High School in Little Rock, Arkansas, Governor Orval Faubus called up the Arkansas National Guard to prevent the black students from entering the building. President Eisenhower, determined to uphold the Supreme Court ruling, sent in U.S. Army troops to escort the black students to their classes. The desegregation of Central High was the first step in a long battle to raise the quality of education for the nation's young black citizens.

Martin Luther King: In addition to government action, individual citizens pushed forward the fight for equal rights between the races. In December 1955 a Montgomery, Alabama woman, Rosa Parks, refused to give up her seat on a city bus to a white passenger. She was arrested. Parks' arrest gave birth to a boycott of the Montgomery city buses by the city's black population. The black community demanded the city transit authority do away with its policy of segregated seating on buses. The Montgomery bus boycott was successful in pushing the United States Supreme Court to outlaw segregated seating on public transportation in 1956. The boycott also brought to the nation's attention a young eloquent Montgomery minister, Martin Luther King, who assumed leadership of the boycott. In the late 1950s, Dr. King would become the preeminent figure in the American civil rights movement. In 1968 he would be assassinated.

John F. Kennedy: On November 8, 1960 John F. Kennedy was elected the thirty-fifth President of the United States. Kennedy came to office with an ambitious social agenda known as the New Frontier. New Frontier legislation and programs: increased the minimum wage, expanded Social Security, and stepped up federal enforcement of the nation's civil rights laws. Yet Kennedy is most remembered for his handling of one key foreign crisis, the Cuban missile crisis.

The Bay of Pigs: When Kennedy entered office in January 1961, he learned that Eisenhower and the Central Intelligence Agency had been planning an invasion of Cuba by CIA trained and equipped Cuban dissidents for the purpose of overthrowing Cuba's communist leader, Fidel Castro. Kennedy decided to go ahead with the plan. On April 17, 1961 the armed dissidents landed at Cuba's Bay of Pigs. Within two days the invasion force was completely defeated by Castro's men after Kennedy refused to send in U.S. air support to aid the invaders. The Bay of Pigs fiasco was a true embarrassment for the United States.

The Cuban Missile Crisis: Undoubtedly because of Kennedy's mishandling of the Bay of Pigs invasion, Soviet leader Nikita Khrushchev decided to test Kennedy's resolve in the summer of 1962. Khrushchev began sending arms to Cuba. Both Khrushchev and Castro claimed the arms were defensive in nature; however, U.S. aerial reconnaissance pictures showed that missiles, capable of reaching U.S. soil, were being installed on Cuba. On October 22, 1962, Kennedy announced to the American public that the Soviet Union had placed offensive missiles on Cuban soil. He also announced that the U.S. had enacted a blockade of the island nation. Khrushchev warned that the Soviet Union would not respect the U.S. blockade.

The U.S. Navy established a wall around Cuba, and U.S. nuclear forces were put on full alert. Eventually, Khrushchev backed down, promising that he would not attempt to place any more missiles on Cuban soil and would remove those missiles which were already in place, if, in turn, the U.S. pledged not to stage any future attacks on Cuba. On October 26, 1962, Kennedy agreed. The Cuban missile crisis was over.

On November 22, 1963, John F. Kennedy was fatally shot while visiting Dallas, Texas, becoming the fourth U.S. President to be assassinated in office. His Vice President, Lyndon Baines Johnson, assumed the Presidency the same day.

Lyndon Baines Johnson: Lyndon Johnson had the most ambitious domestic agenda since Franklin Roosevelt's New Deal. Johnson's Great Society programs dealt mainly with two major problems: racial discrimination and poverty.

Shortly after taking office, Johnson gained passage of the Civil Rights Act of 1964. This act outlawed discrimination in places of public accommodation (i.e. restaurants, stores, hotels, etc.), enabled the federal government to withhold funding from state and local organizations which practiced discrimination, and established the Equal Employment Opportunity Commission (EEOC) to oversee compliance of federal regulations regarding employer-based discrimination. Also in 1964 the Twenty-fourth Amendment to the Constitution was ratified. Prior to the passage of the Twenty-fourth Amendment several southern states required their voters to pay a tax prior to voting. Such poll taxes were designed to keep the poor black citizens of these states from exercising their right to vote. The Twenty-fourth Amendment outlawed this practice.

Great Society programs offered government aid to the elderly and the economically disenfranchised. In 1965 Medicare was enacted which offered federal subsidization of hospital and nursing care for individuals over 65. Akin to Medicare was Medicaid, a federal program designed to provide medical coverage to the nation's poor, regardless of age. Johnson established the Department of Housing and Urban Development to oversee low-income housing and "urban renewal" nationwide. Other Great Society legislation increased the scope of federal job training programs and increased the cash and benefits payments to the nation's poor.

Vietnam: Johnson's domestic agenda soon took a backseat to Vietnam. A former French colony, Vietnam had been overrun by the Japanese in World War II. French attempts to reassert its lost influence in the southeast Asian country after World War II were unsuccessful, and by 1955 France was out of Vietnam for good. Vietnam was left divided into the communist North and the non-communist South. Elections, which were supposed to take place in 1956 to choose a government for a unified Vietnam, were not to be held. The anti-communist leadership of the South, fearing the popularity of the North's communist leader, Ho Chi Minh, refused to hold the elections. The result was Vietnamese Civil War.

The government of South Vietnam would have fallen early on had the United States not come to its aid. Instead of being viewed as just another country undergoing a civil war, Vietnam became the focus of the American policy to contain communism. Under Eisenhower the U.S. supported South Vietnam by sending supplies and military advisors. U.S. support was stepped up during the Kennedy Administration. When Johnson assumed office in November 1963, it became clear that the U.S. would have to become directly involved in the conflict in order to save the South Vietnamese government.

The Gulf of Tonkin Resolution: In August 1964 North Vietnamese patrol boats attacked two U.S. destroyers which were patrolling in the Gulf of Tonkin, just off the coast of North Vietnam. The attacks rallied Congress around Johnson when he went to Capitol Hill with his Gulf of Tonkin Resolution. Congress approved the resolution which gave Johnson carte blanche in Vietnam. Johnson used his blank check to bring the U.S. into the war.

The Vietnam War: U.S. air raids on North Vietnam began in August 1964. The first U.S. ground combat troops arrived in March 1965. By April 1968 the number of U.S. troops peaked at 543,000. The U.S. troops became embroiled in a guerrilla war. Preferring not to take the U.S. troops head-on, the North Vietnamese Army and the South Vietnamese rebels (Viet Cong) engaged in hit and run encounters with the Americans. NVA and Viet Cong troops would make quick strikes against American troops and disappear into the heavily foliated Vietnamese countryside. This guerrilla war culminated in January 1968 with the Tet Offensive during which the North Vietnamese and the Viet Cong launched coordinated guerrilla attacks on American and South Vietnamese forces in Vietnam.

The Home Front: As the war raged in Vietnam a war of a different kind was brewing in the United States. A growing portion of the U.S. population questioned the purpose and morality of U.S. involvement in Vietnam. Television played a major role in the public's perception of the war as the horror of the war was brought into homes across the nation each night. Young women and men of draft age were particularly vocal in their opposition to the war. Demonstrations and draft card burnings took place from coast to coast. Many young males chose to leave the nation rather than fight in the war. A young American of prominence, boxer Cassius Clay, chose to go to prison rather than fight in a war in which he did not believe. The "war" in America climaxed on May 4, 1970. On this day four Kent State students, participating in a campus anti-war demonstration, were shot dead by the Ohio National Guard.

Like the American public, Johnson grew increasingly disillusioned with Vietnam. In March 1968 Johnson announced his intention to begin the de-escalation of American involvement in Vietnam. He also announced that he would not seek reelection in November.

Richard Milhous Nixon: The unpopularity of Vietnam propelled the Republicans and Richard Milhous Nixon to the Presidency in 1968. Nixon was committed to removing U.S. forces from Vietnam. Yet Nixon did not want to be the first U.S. President to lose a war. Consequently, Nixon decided to move slowly in disengaging U.S. forces from the war, wanting to leave the South Vietnamese government in the best possible position to continue the war without the direct assistance of U.S. combat forces. Nixon's policy toward the Vietnam War was known as Vietnamization. Under Vietnamization responsibility for the war was gradually shifted from the U.S. to the government of South Vietnam.

Many believed Nixon was moving too slowly in bringing U.S. troops home. U.S. participation in the war continued several years into his administration. Finally, on January 27, 1973 a cease-fire agreement was signed in Paris by representatives of the U.S., North Vietnam, the Viet Cong, and South Vietnam. The agreement called for the immediate cessation of hostilities and the withdrawal of all remaining U.S. troops.

The Paris accord marked the end of active U.S. involvement in the Vietnam War, but the war itself soon flared up again. South Vietnam was overrun. In April 1975 Saigon, South Vietnam fell. The South Vietnamese government was dismantled. The Vietnam War was over.

Détente: Nixon's greatest accomplishments came in 1972 with his trips to the world's communist superpowers, China and the Soviet Union. Nixon's February trip to China was the first official contact between the two nations for a quarter-century. Even as U.S. troops were fighting communism in Vietnam, just to the south of China, Nixon was meeting with the Chinese communist leaders in an effort to "normalize" relations between the two nations. Nixon's visit marked the beginning of a new and better stage in U.S.-Chinese relations. In May 1972 Nixon traveled to Moscow to meet with Soviet leader Leonid Brezhnev. The two men signed an arms limitation treaty and pledged themselves to "peaceful coexistence." This trip marked the beginning of détente (a lessening of hostilities) between the two rival superpowers.

Watergate: On June 17, 1972 five men were arrested for breaking into the Democratic Party national headquarters in the Watergate office complex in Washington D.C. In March 1973 one of the burglars, James McCord, revealed that his group had not acted alone. According to McCord the Committee to Re-Elect the President, the group responsible for Nixon's 1972 Presidential campaign, was behind the break-in. McCord's testimony had a domino effect which resulted in top members of Nixon's White House staff being implicated in the Watergate break-in and the resulting cover-up.

Throughout the investigation Nixon continued to maintain that he did not authorize, nor have prior knowledge of the Watergate break-in. The Nixon Presidency might have survived had it not been for the Watergate tapes.

The Watergate Tapes: During the Senate investigation of the Watergate break-in, it was revealed that Nixon had taped his top-level meetings in the Oval Office. Nixon refused to hand over his tape library, arguing that "executive privilege" as outlined in the U.S. Constitution gave him the right to keep the tapes private. In July 1974 the Supreme Court ordered Nixon to hand over the tapes.

Nixon complied. After turning over the tapes Nixon admitted that he had known about the Watergate cover-up from the beginning although he did not admit complicity in the initial break-in itself. On August 8, 1974 Nixon resigned.

Gerald Ford: Nixon's replacement, Gerald Ford, had been Nixon's Vice President only since October 1973. Nixon nominated Ford after his original Vice President, Spiro Agnew, was brought down by his own scandal, unrelated to Watergate. An affable man, Ford probably doomed his chance for reelection when he pardoned Nixon from all offenses related to Watergate.

Jimmy Carter: In the 1976 Presidential election Gerald Ford lost to Democrat Jimmy Carter. Carter entered office at a particularly rough time in American history. Americans remained cynical about their government as a result of Vietnam and Watergate. Additionally, the U.S. economy was stricken by both high unemployment and high inflation because of much higher energy prices, courtesy of the Organization of Petroleum Exporting Countries (OPEC). Carter's attempts to improve the economy and deal with the energy crisis were unsuccessful.

The Iranian Hostage Crisis: In 1979 the Middle East nation of Iran underwent a revolution which resulted in the deposition of the U.S. supported Shah. On November 4, 1979 supporters of the revolutionary leader of Iran, Ayatollah Khomeini, seized the U.S. embassy in Tehran and took its staff hostage. For 444 days, 52 Americans remained the unwilling guests of the Iranian government. The fact that U.S. citizens were being held hostage by the government of a third-rate power struck most Americans as unsavory to say the least. Worse, an attempt by Carter to rescue the hostages in April 1980, ended in complete failure.

1981-PRESENT: REAGAN TO TRUMP

The Iranian hostage crisis made Carter look like a truly weak President. Nixon had made many Americans wary of a strong chief executive, but Carter proved weakness was not the answer. On January 20, 1981, Republican Ronald Reagan was inaugurated the fortieth President of the United States. On that same day, Iran released the American hostages.

Ronald Reagan: Ronald Reagan enjoyed a landslide victory in the 1980 Presidential election, garnishing 489 electoral votes compared to 49 for the incumbent Carter. Reagan's answer to the nation's economic woes was supply-side economics which provided a boost to the nation's producers by lowering federal taxes. Also, Reagan pushed for lower government spending, except for defense.

Reaganomics: After tough economic years, 1981 and 1982, the U.S. economy under "Reaganomics" soared. By the end of 1982, the U.S. economy began a non-inflationary economic expansion which would last through the end of Reagan's second term in 1989. When Reagan was elected, the U.S. economy was in recession with high unemployment and an inflation rate of 12.5%. High inflation combined with economic stagnation is known as "stagflation" and it is a dreadful economic situation. Stagflation was hurting Americans everywhere and in November 1980 Carter felt it as well. When Reagan left office in 1989 the economy was growing at 4.2%, unemployment was down substantially, and inflation was 4.4%.

However, prosperity did not come without a cost. Although Reagan succeeded in getting his tax cuts through Congress, he was unsuccessful in reining in Congress and keeping the overall level of federal government spending under control. As a result, the federal government under Reagan experienced unprecedented budget deficits. When Reagan took office in 1981, the federal debt was about $1.0 trillion. By the time Reagan left office in 1989, the federal debt had increased to $2.7 trillion.

Reagan's Cold War Victory: When Reagan assumed office, he began the largest peacetime military build-up in U.S. history. Reagan was determined to do everything he could to undermine the government of the Soviet Union and to stop the spread of communism worldwide. He succeeded. The Soviets attempted and failed to keep pace with Reagan. Their weak Centrally Planned/ Socialist economy was not up to the challenge. Economic pressures resulting from this new, intensified arms race played a decisive role in the fall of the communists and the dissolution of the Soviet Union in the early 1990s.

George H.W. Bush: Reagan's Vice President, George Bush, succeeded him after the 1988 Presidential election. Bush took office at an amazing time in world history. The communist power structure in eastern Europe disintegrated. Countries like Poland and Hungary were born again Democracies. With the collapse of Soviet communism, the focus of U.S. foreign policy shifted from counterbalancing the power of the Soviet Union to maintaining a "new world order."

The Persian Gulf War: The first substantial challenge to Bush's "new world order" foreign policy came in the summer of 1990. On August 2, 1990, Iraqi dictator Sadaam Hussein invaded his smaller, oil-rich neighbor to the south, Kuwait. Bush responded by sending U.S. troops to Saudi Arabia which shared a border with both Kuwait and Iraq. If Hussein decided to push his forces into Saudi Arabia, he would control half of the world's proven petroleum reserves. Bush was determined not to let this happen.

World opinion clearly favored Bush as he took a stand against Hussein's aggression. Troops from the U.S., several European nations, and several Arab nations poured into Saudi Arabia in late 1990. By 1991, the U.S. led coalition forces in the Persian Gulf numbered over 700,000 men and women. On November 29, 1990, Sadaam Hussein was told to leave Kuwait by January 15, 1991, or face forcible eviction.

Hussein refused to capitulate. On January 15, 1991, coalition forces led by U.S. General H. Norman Schwarzkopf launched Operation Desert Storm. For six weeks coalition air power pounded Iraqi forces. By the time Schwarzkopf launched the land invasion of Iraq and Kuwait on February 24, 1991, the shell-shocked Iraqi forces were in no condition to put up much resistance. Within a few days, the fighting was over. The Iraqis accepted surrender terms in early March.

The 1992 Election: The Persian Gulf War victory left Bush immensely popular both at home and abroad. Unfortunately for Bush, over a year and a half separated the end of the war and the 1992 Presidential election. During this period, Bush's popularity plummeted. A somewhat weak economy, the fact that Bush did not keep his "Read my lips: no new taxes" pledge, and the entrance of independent candidate Ross Perot into the Presidential race eroded Bush's support base, enabling Democrat Bill Clinton to capture the Presidency on November 3, 1992, with 43% of the popular vote.

Bill Clinton: During the first two years of his presidency, Bill Clinton seldom enjoyed an approval rating over 50%. His attempt to overhaul the nation's health care system ended in failure. Bill Clinton's unpopularity coupled with a resurgence of American conservatism propelled the Republicans to majorities in both the U.S. Senate and the U.S. House of Representatives after the 1994 congressional elections. Clinton was dogged by sexual misconduct allegations and perjury charges which resulted thereof. He was impeached by the House for perjury and obstruction of justice but later acquitted by the Senate. Clinton, however, did find some success. With Clinton and Congress at each other, Washington was in perpetual gridlock. Being largely left alone, the private sector did quite well. In 2016 dollars, GDP increased from $10.3 trillion in 1992 to $14.0 trillion in 2000.

George W. Bush: On January 20, 2001, George W. Bush, the son of the 41st President of the United States, became the 43rd President. Soon into his term Mr. Bush and the country faced 9/11.

September 11, 2001: On September 11, 2001, the United States of America was attacked. Two hijacked American passenger planes were flown into and brought down the two World Trade Center towers in New York. A third slammed into the Pentagon. 2,977 people were murdered in the attacks. Among these, 343 were FDNY firemen and 40 were the passengers and crew of United Airlines Flight 93 who decided to try to take the cockpit back from the hijackers. The heroic folks of Flight 93 were killed when the hijackers crashed the plane into a field in rural Pennsylvania rather than relinquish the controls. Within hours of the attacks, it became known that the Islamic extremist group Al Qaeda was responsible.

The Wars in Afghanistan and Iraq: Given that Al Qaeda and its odious leader, Osama bin Laden, were holed up in anarchic Afghanistan, the U.S. launched military operations in Afghanistan in late 2001. Military victory was swift. For reasons less clear, Bush also brought the U.S. back to war with Iraq in March 2003. Again, military victory was swift. Iraq's dictator, Sadaam Hussein, went into hiding within a month, was captured by the end of the year, and was tried and hanged by the new Iraqi civilian authority by the end of 2006. Yet, due to persistent and pernicious insurgencies in both theaters, all-out victory in Iraq and Afghanistan has remained elusive even 16 years later. There have been several victories as well as setbacks. In May 2011 the elite U.S. Navy Seals found and terminated bin Laden in his secret compound in the middle of a major city 40 miles from the capital of Pakistan, a supposed U.S. ally in the region. To date, over 4,400 U.S. troops have been killed in Iraq and over 2,300 U.S. troops have been killed in Afghanistan.

At Home: In response to the September 11th attack, Bush and Congress established a new cabinet department, the Department of Homeland Security, and enacted the Patriot Act which many would argue provided security at the expense of some personal liberties. The U.S. mainland remained largely safe for the remainder of his eight-year tenure. The Federal Reserve maintained low interest rates in the wake of the September 11th attack and both the stock and housing market surged, creating a "bubble" in both markets. At the end of Bush's term, the housing bubble popped and took the stock market and the whole U.S. economy with it. The entire U.S. banking system came close to failing because of interdependency and widespread extremely poor housing lending practices. This financial disaster combined with Bush's complete inability (and some would argue unwillingness) to contain excessive domestic government spending, which alienated his base, resulted in the Democrats winning big in 2008.

Barack Obama: The economy tanked in the Fall of 2008 and the Democrats took control of both the Executive and Legislative branches of the federal government. On January 20, 2009, Barack Obama became the 44th President of the United States. Immediately Obama went to work to expand the size and scope of Government.

In February, Obama secured passage of the American Recovery and Reinvestment Act of 2009. It was designed to jumpstart the economy and improve/repair the nation's infrastructure through "shovel-ready" projects, especially in the wake of the 2007 I-35W bridge collapse in Minneapolis, Minnesota. However, of the $800 billion stimulus plan, only $27 billion was set aside for highway and bridge construction and repair. Most of the spending went to shore up state and local government budgets to ensure public sector employee job security, security their private sector counterparts did not share. It should be noted that government employees are a key Democratic Party constituency. Obama and the congressional Democrats then went to work on healthcare. The Patient Protection and Affordable Care Act ("ACA" or "Obamacare") was enacted by Congress and signed into law by Obama on March 23, 2010. Obama's promises to Americans that they would be able to keep their current health insurance plans and doctors, and that their insurance premiums "will go down" would prove to be false.

The Tea Party Movement: Obama's dedication to the expansion of government created a grassroots backlash throughout the country which became known as the Tea Party movement. Although not an officially established party like the Democrats and the Republicans, the Tea Party folks were unified by the belief that government had grown **too big and too intrusive**. As the opposition party and the fact that they at least paid lip service to the idea of smaller government, the Republicans used Tea Party support in the 2010 elections to gain six seats in the Senate and 63 seats in the House where they regained majority status. The Republican's congressional win was their largest in 70 years.

The Debt: The lasting legacy of the Obama presidency was that the U.S. government debt doubled to almost $20 trillion during his term in office (this accounts nothing for future unfunded liabilities primarily in Social Security and Medicare which some argue would add an additional $50 trillion). Aging baby boomers and increasing interest on the existing debt played a role in the creation of this enormous debt bubble, but Obama did nothing to contain, but rather expanded, all government spending. The federal budget went from $2.7 trillion in 2007 to $3.9 trillion in 2016. At the same time, Obama expanded the tax and regulatory burdens on the private sector which, by the way, was tasked with paying for everything.

The Government Bubble: Obama left office in 2017 with a 60% approval rating. His presidency marked the acceleration, but certainly not the start, of government fiscal irresponsibility bordering on insanity. It also begged the question of whether the longtime American ethic of leaving your children with a better life than you yourself experienced was still held by most Americans.

I believe the vast majority of **Americans continue to want a better life for their kids and grandkids**. I also believe that **few Americans truly understand the dire consequences the runaway debt will have down the road**. According to former Joint Chiefs of Staff Chairman Admiral Michael Mullen, "The most significant threat to our national security is our debt."

Many predict that when it is longer in the interest or capability of the rest of the world to buy up an ever-increasing supply of U.S. debt securities, the result will be either **hyperinflation** or **default**. In other words, either the federal government will fire up the "printing presses" and pay off the $20+ trillion with essentially worthless dollars, or the federal government will renege on all its current outstanding debt. Either way, the bursting of the **"Government Bubble"** would have a large and **devastating** impact on the American economy and society.

Federal Government Debt 1900-2016

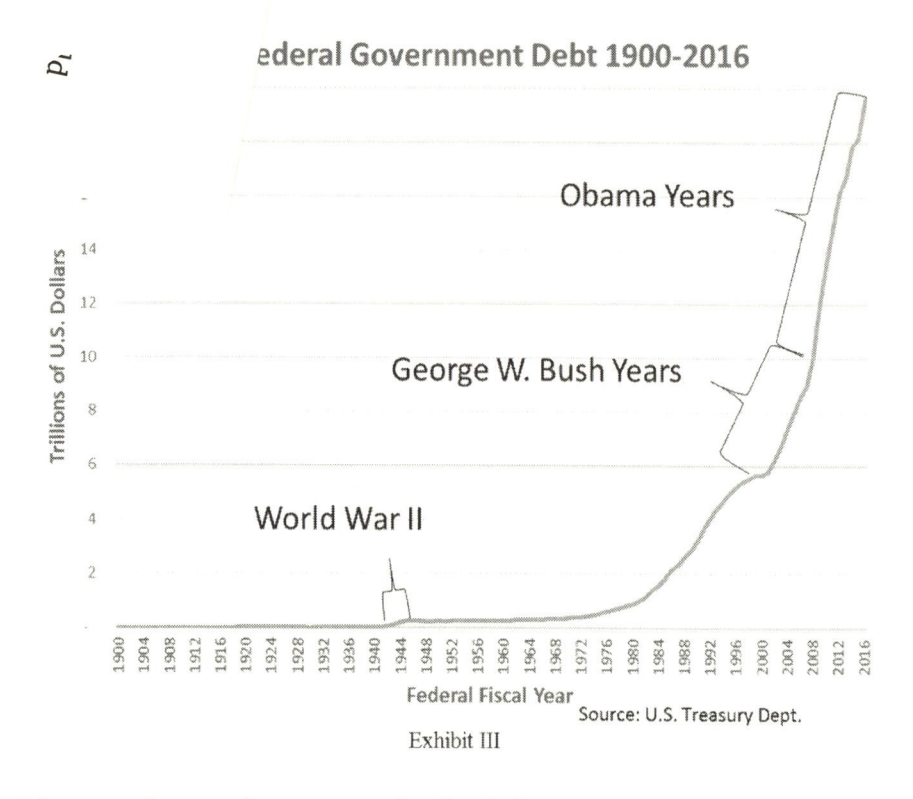

(Trillions of U.S. Dollars, by Federal Fiscal Year)

- Obama Years
- George W. Bush Years
- World War II

Source: U.S. Treasury Dept.

Exhibit III

The one shot we have to gradually deflate the bubble is to **grow the private sector** as much as possible (i.e., increase tax revenues) and **drastically decrease the rate of growth in the public sector** (i.e., cap government spending). This will involve changes to Medicare, Social Security, public sector pensions and all government programs in general. Healthcare changes will have to focus on **cost reduction, instead of benefit expansion**. Government at all levels will have to learn to do more with less. **The public sector will have to learn private sector fiscal discipline**. The electorate thus far has failed to drive home the importance of fiscal discipline to their elected representatives.

Donald Trump: Donald Trump surprised most political pundits with his rise through the Republican primaries and his defeat of former

President Bill Clinton's wife, Hillary, in the general election of 2016. The heart of Donald Trump's campaign was his desire to shift power away from the public sector and back into the hands of the people of the private sector. In other words, he wanted to "**Drain the Swamp**." To Trump, "the Swamp" was a metaphor for all the largely unaccountable big government bureaucrats who had become more concerned with serving their own needs than the needs of the American Citizenry. He planned to achieve this through regulatory reforms such as repealing Obamacare, reforming (i.e. simplifying) the tax code, and cutting taxes. He promised to pursue domestic and foreign policies which made things better for American companies and workers, particularly in manufacturing industries. This was part of Trump's overall **"American First"** message, meaning the President should put the **interests of American citizens above all else** in formulating and implementing domestic and foreign policy. Donald Trump successfully re-engaged many of the same Tea Party folks who were the crucial factor in the 2010 elections. This combined with his appeal to the traditionally Democrat leaning "rust-belt" states of Pennsylvania, Wisconsin, and Michigan propelled Trump to victory.

The Politically Incorrect President: A large part of Trump's appeal was his political incorrectness. In an environment of ever-increasing super-sensitivity and college campuses nationwide which have become **bastions of censorship**, Trump's bluntness and *"call it like he sees it"* persona appealed to many voters. Trump was and is a **disruptor**, what some might call a *"Bull in a China Shop."* In November 2016, U.S. voters decided the D.C. China Shop needed one.

Public Sector Hubris: Another factor in Trump's victory was a growing disdain for what can be called "public sector hubris." Public sector hubris (PSH) is an intangible sense of entitlement among some government workers that really took hold during the Obama years. Public sector workers were largely immune to the economic downturn of 2008-2009. Obama's $800 billion stimulus made sure of that. On the other hand, their private-sector counterparts felt the full force of the recession. Certain (CIVILIAN) public sector employees are very hard to discipline no matter how egregious their conduct or incompetent they may be. IRS Agent Lois Lerner, who targeted conservative groups and individuals for enhanced IRS scrutiny, and Trump targeting FBI Agent Peter Strzok are high-profile examples of this. Whether at the federal, state, or local level, public "servants" who abuse their authority to persecute their political opponents are the **epitome of corruption and tyranny**. Private sector employees, on the other hand, are largely employed "at will." Private sector employees who are not good at their jobs, or simply irk the boss, get fired. Entrepreneurs who are not competent enough or are simply unlucky tend to run out of cash. Trump's victory was partially a backlash to PSH.

PSH does not apply to the soldiers, sailors, or airmen in our military. Also, there are millions of fine police, firemen, border patrolmen, teachers, and other true Public Servants out there. They need to remain vigilant though. PSH is pernicious and contagious. Many of us in the private sector have had enough of it.

The Deep State: Public sector hubris manifests itself in what has become known as the **Deep State**. Deep Staters are entrenched, unelected, and *often insufferably pompous/ smug* bureaucrats who believe that **they are the ones who actually call the shots in government**. Elections and elected representatives of the People come and go, but the Deep Staters only grow more entrenched as time goes by. As long as the President and Congress do not "rock the boat" too much, the Deep Staters are content to rule over their personal power fiefdoms, be it the IRS, the State Department, the

DOJ, or wherever. However, if a popularly elected President were to come along, promising to "**Drain the Swamp**," the Deep Staters would have no hesitation to do everything they could to **undermine that individual**. Also note that the federal Deep Staters have their counterparts at the state and local government levels as well.

You can also throw **activist federal judges** into the Deep State bucket. Appointed for life, rogue federal judges are **almost impossible to remove from the bench**.

Trump's Successes: In his first two years, President Trump enacted numerous regulatory reforms through executive action. Trump followed through with his promise to cut through the regulatory "red tape" the private sector had been forced to fight through during the Obama Administration and before. Trump and Congress cut taxes, but Congress thwarted Trump's attempt to significantly simplify the arcane and inefficient tax code. Trump's lowering of taxes and reforming regulations spurred strong private sector growth. The unemployment rate fell to 3.8% in May 2018, its lowest level in the 21st Century. Through June 2018, the economy was growing at over 4% year over year. President Trump took on trade, renegotiating agreements across the board. He negotiated deals with various trade partners throughout Europe, Asia, and the Americas. Trump made it clear to China that the one-sided U.S.-Chinese trade relationship of the past 15-20 years would be coming to an end, to the **chagrin of the Chinese Communist Party**. Additionally, the Trump Administration enjoyed tremendous success in the ongoing war with radical Islamic terrorist groups such as Al Qaeda and ISIS.

The Deep State Strikes Back: Trump's election caused widespread panic among Hillary Clinton's supporters, not least of which were the Deep State actors who could not fathom life under Trump after eight years of Obama. It appears prominent Deep State actors such as Obama's Director of National Intelligence James Clapper and CIA Director John Brennan used salacious and unsubstantiated **Hillary Clinton Campaign funded** opposition research (hereafter referred to as the "Steele Dossier") to develop and propel a narrative that Trump's victory was illegitimate. This was due to some nebulous and, as it turns out, entirely **FICTITIOUS** conspiracy between Trump and the Russians.

The summer before the election, Brennan and his like-minded colleagues were beginning to grow nervous as Trump was gaining popularity and momentum. It seems they enlisted lower-level FBI Deep State individuals such as Andrew McCabe and the aforementioned Peter Strzok to launch an investigation into whether the Trump Campaign was colluding with the Russians. These individuals **misrepresented** the bogus Steele Dossier to the Foreign Intelligence Surveillance Act (FISA) court to get its authorization to surveil the Trump Campaign. In the wake of 9/11, the ultra-secretive FISA court had been represented to the public as a necessary evil to combat terrorism.

What became known as the Mueller Investigation spent $32 million in taxpayer funds to find exactly nothing pertaining to the Trump Campaign acting illegally (or legally) with any Russians during the 2016 campaign. The only thing of substance that was uncovered was the **deep animosity and contempt the Deep State actors who launched the investigation had for Trump and any Americans who support Trump**. Fortunately, the Deep State actors targeting Trump, although biased and arguably corrupt, were not very bright. Strzok and others (named and unnamed) used their government phones to text their "personal" views. Those "personal" views were made public, and any credibility the Mueller Investigation might once have had with millions of Americans disappeared. The Mueller

Investigation finally came to an **ignominious end** in July 2019 with Robert Mueller's bizarre testimony before Congress where it became clear to anyone with any common sense that the investigation was pretty much a sham from the start.

Trump and the Supreme Court: In his first term, President Trump successfully appointed and had confirmed three justices to the U.S. Supreme Court: Neil Gorsuch, Brett Kavanaugh and Amy Coney Barrett. Trump also successfully filled over 200 federal lower court judicial vacancies. As exemplified by his three Supreme Court appointees, President Trump wanted **Strict Constructionists** (sometimes referred to as **Originalists**) on the court. Strict Constructionists tend to apply the law and the Constitution as written, limiting how far they stretch the meaning of original words and phrases to satisfy specific legal objectives. Also, Strict Constructionists tend to be very protective of individual civil liberties as spelled out in the Bill of Rights (the first ten amendments to the Constitution) and subsequent amendments. Another way of stating this is that they tend to favor **individual rights over government power**. On the other hand, Democrats have tended to support **Liberal** or **Loose Constructionists**. Loose Constructionists tend to stretch the meaning of original words and phrases in the Constitution and subsequent laws to meet particular objectives. At the extreme, Loose Constructionists can be lumped into the aforementioned "activist federal judge" category.

Hunter and Joe Biden: In 2019, Obama's old Vice President, Joe Biden, began to re-emerge on the political scene. Having played a major role as a senator and vice president in the federal bureaucracy (i.e., the DC Swamp) for nearly half a century, Joe Biden established himself as a major player in the **anti-Trump/pro-Swamp** movement. Joe Biden's son, Hunter, is a longtime chronic drug addict who appears to be barely able to manage his personal life. Despite this fact, Hunter was able to secure millions of dollars for a very part-time gig at a corrupt Ukrainian gas company (Burisma Holdings). In December 2013, Hunter travelled to China with his vice president father aboard Air Force Two. Two weeks after the Bidens returned, Hunter's private equity firm announced a **$1.5 billion** private equity deal/ investment with various entities controlled by the Chinese government. Such a deal would typically generate tens of millions of dollars **ANNUALLY** in private equity management fees. The question began to arise, why was the drug-addled Hunter getting all this money? Were these payments to Hunter in fact **backdoor bribes** to Vice President Joe Biden? One of those asking was Donald Trump.

Joe Biden's behavior also stoked the question of impropriety/ corruption. In March 2016, Joe Biden very publicly coerced the Ukrainian government to fire the prosecutor who was investigating Hunter's benefactor, Burisma Holdings. In China's case, Joe's behavior was much more damaging to the American People. In 2001, the Chairman of the Senate Foreign Relations Committee, **Joe Biden, spearheaded China's admission into the World Trade Organization (WTO)**. This was a gamechanger for China which saw its economy grow **eight-fold** from 2001 to 2018. It was also a gamechanger for the U.S. which saw an ever-increasing trade deficit with China and an accompanying transfer of wealth and American manufacturing jobs to China during this same period. Was the **$1.5 billion** a payoff by the Chinese Communist Party to Joe Biden for his past invaluable service and to ensure his future *"friendship"* with Beijing? Many folks, including Trump, began asking this question.

The Impeachment of Donald Trump: In July 2019, President Trump had a "confidential" congratulatory phone call with Ukraine's newly elected president, Volodymyr Zelensky. Trump wanted to address what Zelensky, as a benefactor of U.S. foreign aid, would do to address Ukraine's severe corruption. Trump then mentioned the role Hunter and Joe Biden may have played in Ukraine's past corruption problems. This was enough for Deep State actor Alexander Vindman who was one of the low-level staffers designated to take notes during the call. After the "confidential" call, Vindman and his Deep State colleagues went running to Rep. Adam Schiff (D-CA), another central player in the anti-Trump/pro-Swamp movement. Thus, the gears of impeachment began to grind. Democrats were "appalled" that Trump was using his office to investigate a potential political opponent. Apparently, they had never heard of Lois Lerner, John Brennan, or Peter Strzok. Republicans argued that Trump merely was working to ensure that future **U.S. taxpayer funds** (in the form of foreign aid to Ukraine) would not be **squandered on corrupt payments to unscrupulous characters** like Hunter and Joe Biden. What many called the "Impeachment Hoax" came to an end when the Senate acquitted Trump on February 5, 2020.

As the investigations into President Trump continued, predicated on nothing of substance, tens of millions of Trump voters and some others (e.g., prominent liberal American lawyer Alan Dershowitz) took notice. They began to see the entrenched, unaccountable bureaucratic class (call it the Deep State or whatever) as trying to overrule the will of the American People. When unelected bureaucrats decide that they know better than voters, and therefore should have **unrestricted veto power** over who should be President, we are on **VERY SHAKY GROUND**. This is when **Democracies devolve into Dictatorships**.

COVID-19: While the Democrats were busy with their impeachment, a new threat was emerging in Wuhan, China in the form of what has become known as the **COVID-19 Virus**. Whether

COVID was the result of Chinese Communist Party (CCP) **malice**, or just **incompetence**, is unclear. What is fairly clear is that the COVID virus emerged from a government-run lab in Wuhan in late 2019 and quickly spread throughout the Wuhan area. What is **quite clear** is that the CCP did everything it could to prevent COVID from spreading throughout China, but did **very little** to inform the rest of the world of COVID's extreme contagiousness and **even less** to prevent COVID from escaping China's borders. A reasonable explanation for this is that the CCP figured that if China was being *hobbled* by COVID, then China's rivals, primarily the U.S., needed to be *hobbled* by COVID as well. Also, the CCP undoubtedly figured that spreading COVID to the U.S. would do damage to the **biggest threat** to China's economic and military aspirations, **President Donald Trump**. The fact that China's long-time friend and ally, **Joe Biden**, had emerged as Trump's opponent in the 2020 Election was the *icing on the COVID cake* for the CCP.

The Complicity of the Media/ The Death of Journalism: Throughout the Mueller Investigation, the Impeachment Hoax, and what became utter media hysteria surrounding COVID, the anti-Trump/pro-Swamp movement (Democrats and others) benefitted tremendously from a complicit press and media. Onetime stalwarts of investigative journalism, the New York Times (NYT) and Washington Post (WP), thoroughly covered every allegation made against Trump, no matter how minor or spurious the item. The Mueller Investigation was front page news for two years. When it concluded, revealing no wrongdoing by Trump or anyone with his Campaign, the story was dropped overnight. On the other hand, the NYT and WP **summarily dismissed** credible corruption allegations against Democrats. Credible evidence of Joe Biden's past corruption (best exemplified by the "Hunter Biden Laptop" story) was found unworthy of mention. News organizations of much lesser repute

(CNN, NBC, ABC, etc.) followed the NYT's and the WP's lead. For many, the Times, the Post and others have **devolved** from being **legitimate journalistic institutions** to becoming **vessels of partisan propaganda**. One notable exception is the New York Post, which has shown itself to be determined to delve into allegations of Biden's past corruption.

Aiding the partisans at the NYT and WP, were the partisans at the social media oligopolies, Twitter and Facebook (FB). For four years, Twitter and FB spread allegations and rumors about Trump, regardless of their legitimacy. As Twitter and FB had become the nation's virtual "town squares" folks were largely OK with this as "Freedom of Speech" lies at the heart of what it means to be an American. Yet it became clear to many that Twitter and FB were **not extending that same "Freedom of Speech" to Trump and his supporters**. Testifying before Congress, Twitter's CEO Jack Dorsey and FB's CEO Mark Zuckerberg denied any systematic political bias, blaming any perceived double-standards on some opaque and downright mysterious "algorithms." Yet when the New York Post's "Hunter Biden Laptop" story hit in mid-October 2020, right before the election, Dorsey and Zuckerberg blatantly and openly suppressed it. Any cloak of impartiality evaporated instantly. The First Amendment is not an issue, as both FB and Twitter are private companies. Nevertheless, Twitter's and FB's claims to their users that they were and are open and unbiased forums for discussion were proven to be **FALSE** and **FRAUDULENT**. Both Twitter and FB had become de facto arms of the Biden Campaign, working to secure his election over President Trump.

Of note, one of the **side effects** of the non-stop anti-Trump vitriol generated and disseminated by the Democrat and press/ media alliance were the **Riots of 2020**, beginning in May and continuing up to the election.

The Election of 2020: The Election of 2020 is five days old as of the date of publication of this latest update to my book. As of Election Day night, it appeared Donald Trump had his reelection sewn up. In the subsequent days, more and more ballots for Biden and the Democrats have been added to the tally. Given the reliance on mail-in ballots, precipitated by COVID, this situation is not optimal, but somewhat expected. What has been **unexpected** is the extreme **opacity** with which these ballots have been **gathered** and **tabulated**. Citing COVID concerns, officials in Michigan, Pennsylvania, and elsewhere have kept Republicans and others from observing the process. Given that many of the local officials are very **anti-Trump** (e.g., the governor of Michigan, the mayor of Philadelphia, and the governor and AG of Pennsylvania), many pro-Trump folks smell a rat. Trump supporters look at the Mueller Investigation, the Impeachment of Trump for Biden's corruption, and the non-stop vitriol from the Democrat's political leaders and their media allies, and they come to the conclusion that the Democrats/ Left **will do ANYTHING to gain power**. Would wide-spread vote fraud be that much of a stretch? For tens of millions of Americans, **trust** in these public sector Democrats to conduct legitimate and fair elections **is simply not there**.

The current media narrative is "There's no absolute proof of *'widespread'* vote fraud." It should be noted that it is difficult to produce proof when everything is happening behind closed doors. It is likely the federal courts, including the U.S. Supreme Court, will become increasingly involved. It is unclear, as of now, whether Trump or Biden will prevail. What is abundantly clear is that the Election of 2020 has turned into an **UNMITIGATED MESS**. It seems certain that whoever eventually triumphs in the Election of 2020, the country will emerge from it **more divided than it has been since the 1860s**.

APPENDIX I: THE DECLARATION OF INDEPENDENCE

When in the Course of human events, it becomes necessary for one people to dissolve the political bands which have connected them with another, and to assume among the powers of the earth, the separate and equal station to which the Laws of Nature and of Nature's God entitle them, a decent respect to the opinions of mankind requires that they should declare the causes which impel them to the separation

We hold these truths to be self-evident, that all men are created equal, that they are endowed by their Creator with certain unalienable Rights, that among these are Life, Liberty and the pursuit of Happiness.

That to secure these rights, Governments are instituted among Men, deriving their just powers from the consent of the governed, That whenever any Form of Government becomes destructive of these ends, it is the Right of the People to alter or to abolish it, and to institute new Government, laying its foundation on such principles and organizing its powers in such form, as to them shall seem most likely to effect their Safety and Happiness. Prudence, indeed, will dictate that Governments long established should not be changed for light and transient causes; and accordingly all experience hath shewn, that mankind are more disposed to suffer, while evils are sufferable, than to right themselves by abolishing the forms to which they are accustomed. But when a long train of abuses and usurpations, pursuing invariably the same Object evinces a design to reduce them under absolute Despotism, it is their right, it is their duty, to throw off such Government, and to provide new Guards for their future security.

Such has been the patient sufferance of these Colonies; and such is now the necessity which constrains them to alter their former Systems of Government. The history of the present King of Great Britain is a history of repeated injuries and usurpations, all having in direct object the establishment of an absolute Tyranny over these States. To prove this, let Facts be submitted to a candid world.

> He has refused his Assent to Laws, the most wholesome and necessary for the public good.

He has forbidden his Governors to pass Laws of immediate and pressing importance, unless suspended in their operation till his Assent should be obtained; and when so suspended, he has utterly neglected to attend to them.

He has refused to pass other Laws for the accommodation of large districts of people, unless those people would relinquish the right of Representation in the Legislature, a right inestimable to them and formidable to tyrants only.

He has called together legislative bodies at places unusual, uncomfortable, and distant from the depository of their public Records, for the sole purpose of fatiguing them into compliance with his measures.

He has dissolved Representative Houses repeatedly, for opposing with manly firmness his invasions on the rights of the people.

He has refused for a long time, after such dissolutions, to cause others to be elected; whereby the Legislative Powers, incapable of Annihilation, have returned to the People at large for their exercise; the State remaining in the mean time exposed to all dangers of invasion from without, and convulsions within.

He has endeavored to prevent the population of these States; for that purpose obstructing the Laws of Naturalization of Foreigners; refusing to pass others to encourage their migration hither, and raising the conditions of new Appropriations of Lands.

He has obstructed the Administration of Justice, by refusing his Assent to Laws for establishing Judiciary powers.

He has made Judges dependent on his Will alone, for the tenure of their offices, and the amount and payment of their salaries.

He has erected a multitude of New Offices, and sent hither swarms of Officers to harass our people, and eat out their substance.

He has kept among us, in times of peace, Standing Armies, without the Consent of our legislatures.

He has affected to render the Military independent of and superior to the Civil power.

He has combined with others to subject us to a jurisdiction foreign to our constitution, and unacknowledged by our laws; giving his Assent to their Acts of pretended Legislation:

For Quartering large bodies of armed troops among us:

For protecting them, by a mock Trial, from punishment for any Murders which they should commit on the Inhabitants of these States:

For cutting of our Trade with all parts of the world:

For imposing taxes on us without our Consent:

For depriving us in many cases, of the benefits of Trial by Jury:

For transporting us beyond Seas to be tried for pretended offences:

For abolishing the free System of English Laws in a neighbouring Province, establishing therein an Arbitrary government, and enlarging its Boundaries so as to render it at once an example and fit instrument for introducing the same absolute rule into these Colonies:

For taking away our Charters, abolishing our most valuable Laws, and altering fundamentally the Forms of our Governments:

For suspending our own Legislatures, and declaring themselves invested with power to legislate for us in all cases whatsoever.

He has abdicated Government here, by declaring us out of his Protection and waging War against us.

He has plundered our seas, ravaged our Coasts, burnt our towns, and destroyed the lives of our people.

He is at this time transporting large Armies of foreign Mercenaries to compleat the works of death, desolation and tyranny, already begun with circumstances of Cruelty & perfidy scarcely paralleled in the most barbarous ages, and totally unworthy the Head of a civilized nation.

He has constrained our fellow Citizens taken Captive on the high Seas to bear Arms against their Country, to become the executioners of their friends and Brethren, or to fall themselves by their Hands.

He has excited domestic insurrections amongst us, and has endeavoured to bring on the inhabitants of our frontiers, the merciless Indian Savages, whose known rule of warfare, is an undistinguished destruction of all ages, sexes, and conditions.

In every stage of these Oppressions We have Petitioned for Redress in the most humble terms: Our repeated Petitions have been answered only by repeated injury. A Prince whose character is thus marked by every act which may define a Tyrant, is unfit to be the ruler of a free people.

Nor have We been wanting in attentions to our British brethren. We have warned them from time to time of attempts by their legislature to extend an unwarrantable jurisdiction over us. We have reminded them of the circumstances of our emigration and settlement here. We have appealed to their native justice and magnanimity, and we have conjured them by the ties of our common kindred to disavow these usurpations, which, would inevitably interrupt our connections and correspondence. They too have been deaf to the voice of justice and of consanguinity. We must, therefore, acquiesce in the necessity, which denounces our Separation, and hold them, as we hold the rest of mankind, Enemies in War, in Peace Friends.

We, therefore, the Representatives of the united States of America, in General Congress, Assembled, appealing to the Supreme Judge of the world for the rectitude of our intentions, do, in the Name, and by Authority of the good People of these Colonies, solemnly publish and declare, That these United Colonies are, and of Right ought to be Free and Independent States; that they are Absolved from all Allegiance to the British Crown, and that all political connection between them and the State of Great Britain, is and ought to be totally dissolved; and that as Free and Independent States, they have full Power to levy War, conclude Peace, contract Alliances, establish Commerce, and to do all other Acts and Things which Independent States may of right do. And for the support of this Declaration, with a firm reliance on the Protection of Divine Providence, we mutually pledge to each other our Lives, our Fortunes and our sacred Honor.

APPENDIX II: THE U.S. CONSTITUTION

Preamble

We the People of the United States, in Order to form a more perfect Union, establish Justice, insure domestic Tranquility, provide for the common defence, promote the general Welfare, and secure the Blessings of Liberty to ourselves and our Posterity, do ordain and establish this Constitution for the United States of America.

Article I

Section 1. All legislative Powers herein granted shall be vested in a Congress of the United States, which shall consist of a Senate and House of Representatives.

Section 2. The House of Representatives shall be composed of Members chosen every second Year by the People of the several States, and the Electors in each State shall have the Qualifications requisite for Electors of the most numerous Branch of the State Legislature.

No Person shall be a Representative who shall not have attained to the Age of twenty five Years, and been seven Years a Citizen of the United States, and who shall not, when elected, be an Inhabitant of that State in which he shall be chosen.

Representatives and direct Taxes shall be apportioned among the several States which may be included within this Union, according to their respective Numbers, which shall be determined by adding to the whole Number of free Persons, including those bound to Service for a Term of Years, and excluding Indians not taxed, three fifths of all other Persons. The actual Enumeration shall be made within three Years after the first Meeting of the Congress of the United States, and within every subsequent Term of ten Years, in such Manner as they shall by Law direct. The Number of Representatives shall not exceed one for every thirty Thousand, but each State shall have at Least one Representative; and until such enumeration shall be made, the State of New Hampshire shall be entitled to chuse three, Massachusetts eight, Rhode-Island and Providence Plantations one, Connecticut five, New-York six, New Jersey four, Pennsylvania eight, Delaware one, Maryland six, Virginia ten, North Carolina five, South Carolina five, and Georgia three.

When vacancies happen in the Representation from any State, the Executive Authority thereof shall issue Writs of Election to fill such Vacancies.

The House of Representatives shall chuse their Speaker and other Officers; and shall have the sole Power of Impeachment.

Section 3. The Senate of the United States shall be composed of two Senators from each State, chosen by the Legislature thereof, for six Years; and each Senator shall have one Vote.

Immediately after they shall be assembled in Consequence of the first Election, they shall be divided as equally as may be into three Classes. The Seats of the Senators of the first Class shall be vacated at the Expiration of the second Year, of the second Class at the Expiration of the fourth Year, and of the third Class at the Expiration of the sixth Year, so that one third may be chosen every second Year; and if Vacancies happen by Resignation, or otherwise, during the Recess of the Legislature of any State, the Executive thereof may make temporary Appointments until the next Meeting of the Legislature, which shall then fill such Vacancies.

No Person shall be a Senator who shall not have attained to the Age of thirty Years, and been nine Years a Citizen of the United States, and who shall not, when elected, be an Inhabitant of that State for which he shall be chosen.

The Vice President of the United States shall be President of the Senate, but shall have no Vote, unless they be equally divided.

The Senate shall chuse their other Officers, and also a President pro tempore, in the Absence of the Vice President, or when he shall exercise the Office of President of the United States.

The Senate shall have the sole Power to try all Impeachments. When sitting for that Purpose, they shall be on Oath or Affirmation. When the President of the United States is tried, the Chief Justice shall preside: And no Person shall be convicted without the Concurrence of two thirds of the Members present.

Judgment in Cases of Impeachment shall not extend further than to removal from Office, and disqualification to hold and enjoy any Office of honor, Trust or Profit under the United States: but the Party convicted shall nevertheless be liable and subject to Indictment, Trial, Judgment and Punishment, according to Law.

Section 4. The Times, Places and Manner of holding Elections for Senators and Representatives, shall be prescribed in each State by the Legislature thereof; but the

Congress may at any time by Law make or alter such Regulations, except as to the Places of chusing Senators.

The Congress shall assemble at least once in every Year, and such Meeting shall be on the first Monday in December, unless they shall by Law appoint a different Day.

Section 5. Each House shall be the Judge of the Elections, Returns and Qualifications of its own Members, and a Majority of each shall constitute a Quorum to do Business; but a smaller Number may adjourn from day to day, and may be authorized to compel the Attendance of absent Members, in such Manner, and under such Penalties as each House may provide.

Each House may determine the Rules of its Proceedings, punish its Members for disorderly Behaviour, and, with the Concurrence of two thirds, expel a Member.

Each House shall keep a Journal of its Proceedings, and from time to time publish the same, excepting such Parts as may in their Judgment require Secrecy; and the Yeas and Nays of the Members of either House on any question shall, at the Desire of one fifth of those Present, be entered on the Journal.

Neither House, during the Session of Congress, shall, without the Consent of the other, adjourn for more than three days, nor to any other Place than that in which the two Houses shall be sitting.

Section 6. The Senators and Representatives shall receive a Compensation for their Services, to be ascertained by Law, and paid out of the Treasury of the United States. They shall in all Cases, except Treason, Felony and Breach of the Peace, be privileged from Arrest during their Attendance at the Session of their respective Houses, and in going to and returning from the same; and for any Speech or Debate in either House, they shall not be questioned in any other Place.

No Senator or Representative shall, during the Time for which he was elected, be appointed to any civil Office under the Authority of the United States, which shall have been created, or the Emoluments whereof shall have been encreased during such time; and no Person holding any Office under the United States, shall be a Member of either House during his Continuance in Office.

Section 7. All Bills for raising Revenue shall originate in the House of Representatives; but the Senate may propose or concur with Amendments as on other Bills.

Every Bill which shall have passed the House of Representatives and the Senate, shall, before it become a Law, be presented to the President of the United States; If he approve he shall sign it, but if not he shall return it, with his Objections to that House in which it shall have originated, who shall enter the Objections at large on their Journal, and proceed to reconsider it. If after such Reconsideration two thirds of that House shall agree to pass the Bill, it shall be sent, together with the Objections, to the other House, by which it shall likewise be reconsidered, and if approved by two thirds of that House, it shall become a Law. But in all such Cases the Votes of both Houses shall be determined by yeas and Nays, and the Names of the Persons voting for and against the Bill shall be entered on the Journal of each House respectively. If any Bill shall not be returned by the President within ten Days (Sundays excepted) after it shall have been presented to him, the Same shall be a Law, in like Manner as if he had signed it, unless the Congress by their Adjournment prevent its Return, in which Case it shall not be a Law.

Every Order, Resolution, or Vote to which the Concurrence of the Senate and House of Representatives may be necessary (except on a question of Adjournment) shall be presented to the President of the United States; and before the Same shall take Effect, shall be approved by him, or being disapproved by him, shall be repassed by two thirds of the Senate and House of Representatives, according to the Rules and Limitations prescribed in the Case of a Bill.

Section 8. The Congress shall have Power To lay and collect Taxes, Duties, Imposts and Excises, to pay the Debts and provide for the common Defence and general Welfare of the United States; but all Duties, Imposts and Excises shall be uniform throughout the United States;

To borrow Money on the credit of the United States;

To regulate Commerce with foreign Nations, and among the several States, and with the Indian Tribes;

To establish an uniform Rule of Naturalization, and uniform Laws on the subject of Bankruptcies throughout the United States;

To coin Money, regulate the Value thereof, and of foreign Coin, and fix the Standard of Weights and Measures;

To provide for the Punishment of counterfeiting the Securities and current Coin of the United States;

To establish Post Offices and post Roads;

To promote the Progress of Science and useful Arts, by securing for limited Times to Authors and Inventors the exclusive Right to their respective Writings and Discoveries;

To constitute Tribunals inferior to the supreme Court;

To define and punish Piracies and Felonies committed on the high Seas, and Offences against the Law of Nations;

To declare War, grant Letters of Marque and Reprisal, and make Rules concerning Captures on Land and Water;

To raise and support Armies, but no Appropriation of Money to that Use shall be for a longer Term than two Years;

To provide and maintain a Navy;

To make Rules for the Government and Regulation of the land and naval Forces;

To provide for calling forth the Militia to execute the Laws of the Union, suppress Insurrections and repel Invasions;

To provide for organizing, arming, and disciplining, the Militia, and for governing such Part of them as may be employed in the Service of the United States, reserving to the States respectively, the Appointment of the Officers, and the Authority of training the Militia according to the discipline prescribed by Congress;

To exercise exclusive Legislation in all Cases whatsoever, over such District (not exceeding ten Miles square) as may, by Cession of particular States, and the Acceptance of Congress, become the Seat of the Government of the United States, and to exercise like Authority over all Places purchased by the Consent of the Legislature of the State in which the Same shall be, for the Erection of Forts, Magazines, Arsenals, dock-Yards, and other needful Buildings;-And

To make all Laws which shall be necessary and proper for carrying into Execution the foregoing Powers, and all other Powers vested by this Constitution in the Government of the United States, or in any Department or Officer thereof.

Section. 9. The Migration or Importation of such Persons as any of the States now existing shall think proper to admit, shall not be prohibited by the Congress prior to the Year one thousand eight hundred and eight, but a Tax or duty may be imposed on such Importation, not exceeding ten dollars for each Person.

The Privilege of the Writ of Habeas Corpus shall not be suspended, unless when in Cases of Rebellion or Invasion the public Safety may require it.

No Bill of Attainder or ex post facto Law shall be passed.

No Capitation, or other direct, Tax shall be laid, unless in Proportion to the Census or enumeration herein before directed to be taken.

No Tax or Duty shall be laid on Articles exported from any State.

No Preference shall be given by any Regulation of Commerce or Revenue to the Ports of one State over those of another: nor shall Vessels bound to, or from, one State, be obliged to enter, clear, or pay Duties in another.

No Money shall be drawn from the Treasury, but in Consequence of Appropriations made by Law; and a regular Statement and Account of the Receipts and Expenditures of all public Money shall be published from time to time.

No Title of Nobility shall be granted by the United States: And no Person holding any Office of Profit or Trust under them, shall, without the Consent of the Congress, accept of any present, Emolument, Office, or Title, of any kind whatever, from any King, Prince, or foreign State.

Section. 10. No State shall enter into any Treaty, Alliance, or Confederation; grant Letters of Marque and Reprisal; coin Money; emit Bills of Credit; make any Thing but gold and silver Coin a Tender in Payment of Debts; pass any Bill of Attainder, ex post facto Law, or Law impairing the Obligation of Contracts, or grant any Title of Nobility.

No State shall, without the Consent of the Congress, lay any Imposts or Duties on Imports or Exports, except what may be absolutely necessary for executing it's inspection Laws: and the net Produce of all Duties and Imposts, laid by any State on Imports or Exports, shall be for the Use of the Treasury of the United States; and all such Laws shall be subject to the Revision and Controul of the Congress.

No State shall, without the Consent of Congress, lay any Duty of Tonnage, keep Troops, or Ships of War in time of Peace, enter into any Agreement or Compact with another State, or with a foreign Power, or engage in War, unless actually invaded, or in such imminent Danger as will not admit of delay.

Article II

Section. 1. The executive Power shall be vested in a President of the United States of America. He shall hold his Office during the Term of four Years, and, together with the Vice President, chosen for the same Term, be elected, as follows:

Each State shall appoint, in such Manner as the Legislature thereof may direct, a Number of Electors, equal to the whole Number of Senators and Representatives to which the State may be entitled in the Congress: but no Senator or Representative, or Person holding an Office of Trust or Profit under the United States, shall be appointed an Elector.

The Electors shall meet in their respective States, and vote by Ballot for two Persons, of whom one at least shall not be an Inhabitant of the same State with themselves. And they shall make a List of all the Persons voted for, and of the Number of Votes for each; which List they shall sign and certify, and transmit sealed to the Seat of the Government of the United States, directed to the President of the Senate. The President of the Senate shall, in the Presence of the Senate and House of Representatives, open all the Certificates, and the Votes shall then be counted. The Person having the greatest Number of Votes shall be the President, if such Number be a Majority of the whole Number of Electors appointed; and if there be more than one who have such Majority, and have an equal Number of Votes, then the House of Representatives shall immediately chuse by Ballot one of them for President; and if no Person have a Majority, then from the five highest on the List the said House shall in like Manner chuse the President. But in chusing the President, the Votes shall be taken by States, the Representation from each State having one Vote; A quorum for this Purpose shall consist of a Member or Members from two thirds of the States, and a Majority of all the States shall be necessary to a Choice. In every Case, after the Choice of the President, the Person having the greatest Number of Votes of the Electors shall be the Vice President. But if there should remain two or more who have equal Votes, the Senate shall chuse from them by Ballot the Vice President.

The Congress may determine the Time of chusing the Electors, and the Day on which they shall give their Votes; which Day shall be the same throughout the United States.

No Person except a natural born Citizen, or a Citizen of the United States, at the time of the Adoption of this Constitution, shall be eligible to the Office of President; neither shall any Person be eligible to that Office who shall not have attained to the Age of thirty five Years, and been fourteen Years a Resident within the United States.

In Case of the Removal of the President from Office, or of his Death, Resignation, or Inability to discharge the Powers and Duties of the said Office, the Same shall devolve on the Vice President, and the Congress may by Law provide for the Case of Removal, Death, Resignation or Inability, both of the President and Vice President, declaring what Officer shall then act as President, and such Officer shall act accordingly, until the Disability be removed, or a President shall be elected.

The President shall, at stated Times, receive for his Services, a Compensation, which shall neither be encreased nor diminished during the Period for which he shall have been elected, and he shall not receive within that Period any other Emolument from the United States, or any of them.

Before he enter on the Execution of his Office, he shall take the following Oath or Affirmation:-"I do solemnly swear (or affirm) that I will faithfully execute the Office of President of the United States, and will to the best of my Ability, preserve, protect and defend the Constitution of the United States."

Section. 2. The President shall be Commander in Chief of the Army and Navy of the United States, and of the Militia of the several States, when called into the actual Service of the United States; he may require the Opinion, in writing, of the principal Officer in each of the executive Departments, upon any Subject relating to the Duties of their respective Offices, and he shall have Power to grant Reprieves and Pardons for Offences against the United States, except in Cases of Impeachment.

He shall have Power, by and with the Advice and Consent of the Senate, to make Treaties, provided two thirds of the Senators present concur; and he shall nominate, and by and with the Advice and Consent of the Senate, shall appoint Ambassadors, other public Ministers and Consuls, Judges of the supreme Court, and all other Officers of the United States, whose Appointments are not herein otherwise provided for, and which shall be established by Law: but the Congress may by Law vest the Appointment of such inferior Officers, as they think proper, in the President alone, in the Courts of Law, or in the Heads of Departments.

The President shall have Power to fill up all Vacancies that may happen during the Recess of the Senate, by granting Commissions which shall expire at the End of their next Session.

Section. 3. He shall from time to time give to the Congress Information of the State of the Union, and recommend to their Consideration such Measures as he shall judge necessary and expedient; he may, on extraordinary Occasions, convene both Houses, or either of them, and in Case of Disagreement between them, with Respect to the Time of Adjournment, he may adjourn them to such Time as he shall think proper;

he shall receive Ambassadors and other public Ministers; he shall take Care that the Laws be faithfully executed, and shall Commission all the Officers of the United States.

Section. 4. The President, Vice President and all civil Officers of the United States, shall be removed from Office on Impeachment for, and Conviction of, Treason, Bribery, or other high Crimes and Misdemeanors.

Article III

Section. 1. The judicial Power of the United States, shall be vested in one supreme Court, and in such inferior Courts as the Congress may from time to time ordain and establish. The Judges, both of the supreme and inferior Courts, shall hold their Offices during good Behaviour, and shall, at stated Times, receive for their Services, a Compensation, which shall not be diminished during their Continuance in Office.

Section. 2. The judicial Power shall extend to all Cases, in Law and Equity, arising under this Constitution, the Laws of the United States, and Treaties made, or which shall be made, under their Authority;—to all Cases affecting Ambassadors, other public Ministers and Consuls;—to all Cases of admiralty and maritime Jurisdiction;—to Controversies to which the United States shall be a Party;—to Controversies between two or more States;— between a State and Citizens of another State,—between Citizens of different States,—between Citizens of the same State claiming Lands under Grants of different States, and between a State, or the Citizens thereof, and foreign States, Citizens or Subjects.

In all Cases affecting Ambassadors, other public Ministers and Consuls, and those in which a State shall be Party, the supreme Court shall have original Jurisdiction. In all the other Cases before mentioned, the supreme Court shall have appellate Jurisdiction, both as to Law and Fact, with such Exceptions, and under such Regulations as the Congress shall make.

The Trial of all Crimes, except in Cases of Impeachment, shall be by Jury; and such Trial shall be held in the State where the said Crimes shall have been committed; but when not committed within any State, the Trial shall be at such Place or Places as the Congress may by Law have directed.

Section. 3. Treason against the United States, shall consist only in levying War against them, or in adhering to their Enemies, giving them Aid and Comfort. No Person shall be convicted of Treason unless on the Testimony of two Witnesses to the same overt Act, or on Confession in open Court.

The Congress shall have Power to declare the Punishment of Treason, but no Attainder of Treason shall work Corruption of Blood, or Forfeiture except during the Life of the Person attainted.

Article IV

Section. 1. Full Faith and Credit shall be given in each State to the public Acts, Records, and judicial Proceedings of every other State. And the Congress may by general Laws prescribe the Manner in which such Acts, Records and Proceedings shall be proved, and the Effect thereof.

Section. 2. The Citizens of each State shall be entitled to all Privileges and Immunities of Citizens in the several States.

A Person charged in any State with Treason, Felony, or other Crime, who shall flee from Justice, and be found in another State, shall on Demand of the executive Authority of the State from which he fled, be delivered up, to be removed to the State having Jurisdiction of the Crime.

No Person held to Service or Labour in one State, under the Laws thereof, escaping into another, shall, in Consequence of any Law or Regulation therein, be discharged from such Service or Labour, but shall be delivered up on Claim of the Party to whom such Service or Labour may be due.

Section. 3. New States may be admitted by the Congress into this Union; but no new State shall be formed or erected within the Jurisdiction of any other State; nor any State be formed by the Junction of two or more States, or Parts of States, without the Consent of the Legislatures of the States concerned as well as of the Congress.

The Congress shall have Power to dispose of and make all needful Rules and Regulations respecting the Territory or other Property belonging to the United States; and nothing in this Constitution shall be so construed as to Prejudice any Claims of the United States, or of any particular State.

Section. 4. The United States shall guarantee to every State in this Union a Republican Form of Government, and shall protect each of them against Invasion; and on Application of the Legislature, or of the Executive (when the Legislature cannot be convened), against domestic Violence.

Article V

The Congress, whenever two thirds of both Houses shall deem it necessary, shall propose Amendments to this Constitution, or, on the Application of the Legislatures of two thirds of the several States, shall call a Convention for proposing Amendments, which, in either Case, shall be valid to all Intents and Purposes, as Part of this Constitution, when ratified by the Legislatures of three fourths of the several States, or by Conventions in three fourths thereof, as the one or the other Mode of Ratification may be proposed by the Congress; Provided that no Amendment which may be made prior to the Year One thousand eight hundred and eight shall in any Manner affect the first and fourth Clauses in the Ninth Section of the first Article; and that no State, without its Consent, shall be deprived of its equal Suffrage in the Senate.

Article VI

All Debts contracted and Engagements entered into, before the Adoption of this Constitution, shall be as valid against the United States under this Constitution, as under the Confederation.

This Constitution, and the Laws of the United States which shall be made in Pursuance thereof; and all Treaties made, or which shall be made, under the Authority of the United States, shall be the supreme Law of the Land; and the Judges in every State shall be bound thereby, any Thing in the Constitution or Laws of any State to the Contrary notwithstanding.

The Senators and Representatives before mentioned, and the Members of the several State Legislatures, and all executive and judicial Officers, both of the United States and of the several States, shall be bound by Oath or Affirmation, to support this Constitution; but no religious Test shall ever be required as a Qualification to any Office or public Trust under the United States.

Article VII

The Ratification of the Conventions of nine States, shall be sufficient for the Establishment of this Constitution between the States so ratifying the Same.

Amendments to the Constitution of the United States

"Resolved, By the Senate and the House of Representatives of the United States of America, in congress assembled, two-thirds of both Houses concurring, that the following articles be proposed to the Legislatures of the several States, as amendments to the Constitution of the United States; all or any of which articles, when ratified by three-fourths of the said Legislatures, to be valid to all intents and purposes, as part of the said Constitution, namely:"

The Bill of Rights (1791)

Amendment I- Congress shall make no law respecting an establishment of religion, or prohibiting the free exercise thereof; or abridging the freedom of speech, or of the press; or the right of the people peaceably to assemble, and to petition the Government for a redress of grievances.

Amendment II- A well-regulated Militia, being necessary to the security of a free State, the right of the people to keep and bear arms, shall not be infringed.

Amendment III- No soldier shall, in time of peace be quartered in any house, without the consent of the Owner, nor in time of war, but in a manner to be prescribed by law.

Amendment IV- The right of the people to be secure in their persons, houses, papers, and effects, against unreasonable searches and seizures, shall not be violated, and no Warrants shall issue, but upon probable cause, supported by Oath or affirmation, and particularly describing the place to be searched, and the persons or things to be seized.

Amendment V- No person shall be held to answer for a capital, or otherwise infamous crime, unless on a presentment or indictment of a Grand Jury, except in cases arising in the land or naval forces, or in the Militia, when in actual service in time of War or public danger; nor shall any person be subject for the same offence to be twice put in jeopardy of life or limb; nor shall be compelled in any criminal case to be a witness against himself, nor be deprived of life, liberty, or property, without due process of law; nor shall private property be taken for public use, without just compensation.

Amendment VI- In all criminal prosecutions, the accused shall enjoy the right to a speedy and public trial, by an impartial jury of the State and district wherein the crime shall have been committed, which district shall have been previously ascertained by law, and to be informed of the nature and cause of the accusation; to be confronted with the witnesses against him; to have compulsory process for obtaining witnesses in his favor, and to have the Assistance of Counsel for his defence.

Amendment VII- In Suits at common law, where the value in controversy shall exceed twenty dollars, the right of trial by jury shall be preserved, and no fact tried by a jury, shall be otherwise reexamined in any court of the United States, than according to the rules of the common law.

Amendment VIII- Excessive bail shall not be required, nor excessive fines imposed, nor cruel and unusual punishments inflicted.

Amendment IX- The enumeration in the Constitution, of certain rights, shall not be construed to deny or disparage others retained by the people.

Amendment X- The powers not delegated to the United States by the Constitution, nor prohibited by it to the States, are reserved to the States respectively, or to the people.

Subsequent Amendments

Amendment XI- (1798)- The Judicial power of the United States shall not be construed to extend to any suit in law or equity, commenced or prosecuted against one of the United States by Citizens of another State, or by Citizens or Subjects of any Foreign State.

Amendment XII- (1804)- The Electors shall meet in their respective states and vote by ballot for President and Vice President, one of whom, at least, shall not be an inhabitant of the same State with themselves; they shall name in their ballots the person voted for as President, and in distinct ballots the person voted for as Vice President; and they shall make distinct lists of all persons voted for as President, and of all persons voted for as Vice President, and of the number of votes for each, which list they shall sign and certify, and transmit, sealed, to the seat of the Government of the United States, directed to the President of the Senate;- The President of the Senate shall, in the presence of the Senate and the House of Representatives, open all the certificates and the votes shall then be counted;- The person having the greatest number of votes for President, shall be the President, if such number be a majority of the whole number of Electors appointed; and if no persons have such majority, then from the persons having the highest numbers not exceeding three on the list of those voted for as President, the House of Representatives shall choose immediately, by ballot, the President. But in choosing the President, the votes shall be taken by States, the representation from each State having one vote; a quorum for this purpose shall consist of a member or members from two-thirds of the States, and a majority of all the States shall be necessary to a choice. And if the House of Representatives shall not choose a President whenever the right of choice shall devolve upon them, before the fourth day of March next following, then the Vice President shall act as President, as in the case of the death or other constitutional disability of the President. The person having the greatest number of votes as Vice

President, shall be the Vice President, if such number be a majority of the whole number of Electors appointed, and if no person have a majority, then from the two highest numbers on the list, the Senate shall choose the Vice President; a quorum for the purpose shall consist of two-thirds of the whole number of Senators, and a majority of the whole number shall be necessary to a choice. But no person constitutionally ineligible to the office of President shall be eligible to that of Vice President of the United States.

Amendment XIII- (1865)- 1. Neither slavery nor involuntary servitude, except as a punishment for a crime whereof the party shall have been duly convicted, shall exist within the United States, or any place subject to their jurisdiction. 2. Congress shall have power to enforce this article by appropriate legislation.

Amendment XIV- (1868)- 1. All persons born or naturalized in the United States and subject to the jurisdiction thereof, are citizens of the United States and of the State wherein they reside. No State shall make or enforce any law which shall abridge the privileges or immunities of citizens of the United States; nor shall any State deprive any person of life, liberty, or property, without due process of law; nor deny to any person within its jurisdiction the equal protection of the laws.

2. Representatives shall be apportioned among the several States according to their respective numbers, counting the whole number of persons in each State, excluding Indians not taxed. But when the right to vote at any election for the choice of electors for President and Vice President of the United States, Representatives in Congress, the Executive and Judicial officers of a State, or the members of the Legislature thereof, is denied to any of the male members of such State, being of twenty-one years of age, and citizens of the United States, or in any way abridged, except for participation in rebellion or other crime, the basis of representation therein shall be reduced in the proportion which the number of such male citizens shall bear to the whole number of male citizens twenty-one years of age in such State.

3. No person shall be a Senator or Representative in Congress, or elector of President and Vice President, or hold any office, civil or, military, under the United States, or under any State, who, having previously taken an oath as a member of Congress, or as an officer of the United States, or as a member of any State Legislature, or as an executive or judicial officer of any State, to support the Constitution of the United States, shall have engaged in insurrection or rebellion against the same, or given aid or comfort to the enemies thereof. But Congress may, by a vote of two-thirds of each House, remove such disability.

4. The validity of the public debt of the United States, authorized by law, including debts incurred for payment of pensions and bounties for services in suppressing

insurrection or rebellion, shall not be questioned. But neither the United States nor any State shall assume or pay any debt or obligation incurred in aid of insurrection or rebellion against the United States, or any claim for the loss or emancipation of any slave; but all such debts, obligations and claims shall be held illegal and void.

5. The Congress shall have power to enforce, by appropriate legislation, the provisions of this article.

Amendment XV- (1870)- 1. The right of the citizens of the United States to vote shall not be denied or abridged by the United States or by any State on account of race, color, or previous condition of servitude. 2. The Congress shall have power to enforce this article by appropriate legislation.

Amendment XVI- (1913)- The Congress shall have power to lay and collect taxes on incomes, from whatever sources derived, without apportionment among the several States, and without regard to any census or enumeration.

Amendment XVII- (1913)- 1. The Senate of the United States shall be composed of two Senators from each State, elected by the people thereof, for six years; and each Senator shall have one vote. The electors in each State shall have the qualifications requisite for electors of the most numerous branch of the State Legislatures.

2. When vacancies happen in the representation of any State in the Senate, the executive authority of such State shall issue writs of election fill such vacancies; Provided, That the Legislature of any State may empower the Executive thereof to make temporary appointment until the people fill the vacancies by election as the Legislature may direct.

3. This amendment shall not be so construed as to affect the election or term of any Senator chosen before it becomes valid as part of the Constitution.

Amendment XVIII- (1919)- 1. After one year from the ratification of this article the manufacture, sale, or transportation of intoxicating liquors within, the importation thereof into, or the exportation thereof from the United States and all territory subject to the jurisdiction thereof for beverage purposes is hereby prohibited.

2. The Congress and the several States shall have concurrent power to enforce this article by appropriate legislation.

3. This article shall be inoperative unless it shall have been ratified as an amendment to the Constitution by the Legislatures of the several States, as provided in the Constitution, within seven years from the date of the submission hereof to the States by the Congress.

Amendment XIX- (1920)- The right of citizens of the United States to vote shall not be denied or abridged by the United States or by any State on account of sex. Congress shall have power to enforce this article by appropriate legislation.

Amendment XX- (1933)- 1. The terms of the President and Vice President shall end at noon on the 20th day of January, and the terms of Senators and Representatives at noon on the 3rd day of January, of the years in which such terms would have ended if this article had not been ratified; and the terms of their successors shall then begin.

2. The Congress shall assemble at least once in every year, and such meeting shall begin at noon on the 3rd day of January, unless they shall by law appoint a different day.

3. If, at the time fixed for the beginning of a term of the President, the President elect shall have died, the Vice President elect shall become President. If a President shall not have been chosen before the time fixed for the beginning of his term, or if the President elect shall have failed to qualify, then the Vice President elect shall act as President until a President shall have qualified; and the Congress may by law provide for the case wherein neither a President elect nor a Vice President elect shall have qualified, declaring who shall then act as President, or the manner in which one who is to act shall be selected, and such person shall act accordingly until a President or Vice President shall have qualified.

4. The Congress may by law provide for the case of the death of any of the persons from whom the House of Representatives may choose a President whenever the right of choice shall have devolved upon them, and for the case of the death of any of the persons from whom the Senate may choose a Vice President whenever the right of choice shall have devolved upon them.

5. Sections 1 and 2 shall take effect on the 15th day of October following the ratification of this article.

6. This article shall be inoperative unless it shall have been ratified as an amendment to the Constitution by the legislatures of three fourths of the several States within seven years from the date of its submission.

Amendment XXI- (1933)- 1. The eighteenth article of amendment to the Constitution of the United States is hereby repealed.

2. The transportation or importation into any State, Territory, or possession of the United States for delivery or use therein of intoxicating liquors, in violation of the laws thereof, is hereby prohibited.

3. This article shall be inoperative unless it shall have been ratified as an amendment to the Constitution by conventions in the several States, as provided in the

Constitution, within seven years from the date of the submission hereof to the States by the Congress.

Amendment XXII- (1951)- 1. No person shall be elected to the office of the President more than twice, and no person who has held the office of President, or acted as President, for more than two years of a term to which some other person was elected President shall be elected to the office of President more than once. But this Article shall not apply to any person holding the office of President when this Article was proposed by the Congress, and shall not prevent any person who may be holding the office of President, or acting as President, during the term within which this Article becomes operative from holding the office of President or acting as President during the remainder of such term.

2. This article shall be inoperative unless it shall have been ratified as an amendment to the Constitution by the legislatures of three-fourths of the several States within seven years from the date of its submission to the States by the Congress.

Amendment XXIII- (1961)- 1. The District constituting the seat of Government of the United States shall appoint in such manner as the Congress may direct: A number of electors of President and Vice President equal to the whole number of Senators and Representatives in Congress to which the District would be entitled if it were a State, but in no event more than the least populous State; they shall be in addition to those appointed by the States, but they shall be considered, for the purposes of the election of President and Vice President, to be electors appointed by a State; and they shall meet in the District and perform such duties as provided by the twelfth article of amendment. 2. The Congress shall have power to enforce this article by appropriate legislation.

Amendment XXIV- (1964)- 1. The right of citizens of the United States to vote in any primary or other election for President or Vice President, for electors for President or Vice President, or for Senator or Representative in Congress, shall not be denied or abridged by the United States or any State by reason of failure to pay any poll tax or other tax. 2. The Congress shall have power to enforce this article by appropriate legislation.

Amendment XXV- (1967)- 1. In case of the removal of the President from office or of his death or resignation, the Vice President shall become President.

2. Whenever there is a vacancy in the office of the Vice President, the President shall nominate a Vice President who shall take office upon confirmation by a majority vote of both Houses of Congress.

3. Whenever the President transmits to the President pro tempore of the Senate and the Speaker of the House of Representatives his written declaration that he is unable

to discharge the powers and duties of his office, and until he transmits to them a written declaration to the contrary, such powers and duties shall be discharged by the Vice President as Acting President.

4. Whenever the Vice President and a majority of either the principal officers of the executive departments or of such other body as Congress may by law provide, transmit to the President pro tempore of the Senate and the Speaker of the House of Representatives their written declaration that the President is unable to discharge the powers and duties of his office, the Vice President shall immediately assume the powers and duties of the office as Acting President.

Thereafter, when the President transmits to the President pro tempore of the Senate and the Speaker of the House of Representatives his written declaration that no inability exists, he shall resume the powers and duties of his office unless the Vice President and a majority of either the principal officers of the executive department or of such other body as Congress may by law provide, transmit within four days to the President pro tempore of the Senate and the Speaker of the House of Representatives their written declaration that the President is unable to discharge the powers and duties of his office. Thereupon Congress shall decide the issue, assembling within forty-eight hours for that purpose if not in session. If the Congress, within twenty-one days after receipt of the latter written declaration, or, if Congress is not in session, within twenty-one days after Congress is required to assemble, determines by two-thirds vote of both Houses that the President is unable to discharge the powers and duties of his office, the Vice President shall continue to discharge the same as Acting President; otherwise, the President shall resume the powers and duties of his office.

Amendment XXVI- (1971)- 1. The right of citizens of the United States, who are eighteen years of age or older, to vote shall not be denied or abridged by the United States or by any State on account of age. 2. The Congress shall have power to enforce this article by appropriate legislation.

Amendment XXVII- (1992)- 1. No law, varying the compensation for the services of the Senators and Representatives, shall take effect, until an election of Representatives shall have intervened.

Made in the USA
Middletown, DE
11 March 2021